Blueprint
TWO

Students' Book

Brian Abbs
Ingrid Freebairn

Longman

Contents

Preview

UNITS 1–5

🎧 Listen and follow the text.

1 My name is Clare Taylor. I live in Oxford but work in London. I'm the director of an employment agency called 'Work International'. We help people to find work abroad.

2 I'm Josh Kumar. I've got an interview today at Work International. I'm hoping to get a job as a tour guide in Europe.

Interested in working abroad?

Are you looking for a job abroad? We have exciting jobs as tour guides, children's camp leaders, sports instructors, etc.
If you are interested write to Clare Taylor at:

**Work International,
98, Stratford Street,
London E14 9TE.**

Tel: 071-987 09156

Answer the questions.

1 Where does Clare Taylor live?
2 What does she do?
3 What sort of job does Josh want?
4 Where does Lisa come from?
5 Where is she going to stay?
6 Where does Bob come from?
7 How many children has he got?

In Units 1–5 you will revise the main verb tenses and you will also learn how to:

– introduce yourself
– give details of your life so far
– talk about likes and dislikes
– agree and disagree
– say how often you do things
– describe people and places

FAMILY

Got any brothers or sisters?   How many?

ROUTINES

What time/usually get up/morning?
What/usually have/breakfast?

READING HABITS

What newspaper/read every day?
What magazines/usually buy?

PRESENT ACTIVITIES

What book/read/at the moment?
What other languages/learn?

-1-
About you

1 ▣ DIALOGUE

JOSH: Oh, good morning. My name's Josh Kumar. I've got an interview with Clare Taylor at half past nine.

WOMAN: Oh yes, hello. Can you fill in this questionnaire, please?

JOSH: Sure. . . .

CLARE: Goodbye, Adam. I hope it goes well in Mexico.

ADAM: Thanks. Bye! . . .

CLARE: Ah! How do you do, Mr Kumar? I'm Clare Taylor. Nice to meet you.

JOSH: How do you do?

Listen and answer the questions.

1 What does the receptionist say to greet Josh?
2 What does Clare say to greet Josh?
3 Who is more formal, the receptionist or Clare?

2 Introduce yourself in different ways to other people in the class.

A: Hello. My name's (Paul Marten).
B: Hello. I'm (Carla Metz). Nice to meet you.

FUTURE PLANS

What/going to do this evening?
What/going to do at the weekend?

BIRTHDAYS

When/be/your birthday?
What/usually do/your birthday?

INTERESTS AND SPORTS

What/like doing/spare time?   What music/like?
Play any sports?   Which?

LAST NIGHT

What/do last night?   What time/go to bed?

HOLIDAYS

Where/go/last summer holiday?   Where/stay?

EXPERIENCES

Ever be/Britain or the USA?
Ever live/foreign country?

3 Ask questions from the questionnaire. Make a note of your partner's answers.

A: Have you got any brothers or sisters?
B: Yes, I've got two sisters and a brother. What about you?
A: I've got a brother. I haven't got any sisters.

4 Tell the class about some of the things you have in common with your partner.

Both of us have got a brother. **Neither** of us gets up early.

GRAMMAR FOCUS: Revision of tenses

Present simple
Where do you live?
I live in Madrid.

Present continuous
What are you doing?
I'm writing a letter.

Have got
Have you got any brothers?
Yes, I've got one brother.

Going to future
What are you going to do this weekend?
I'm going to stay at home.

Past simple
What did you do last night?
I went to the cinema.

Present perfect simple
Have you ever been to Scotland?
No, I haven't but I've been to Ireland.

5 Clare's Australian niece, Lisa, is in Germany. Complete her letter to Clare by writing the correct form of the verb in brackets.

Munich
Germany
Sunday, 20th June

Dear Clare,

I (leave) Australia at the end of April and I (get) closer to Britain every day! I (arrive) in Munich two days ago and I now (stay) with my German penfriend, Suzanne, and her family. They (have got) a flat near the centre of Munich.

Suzanne (have got) a job with a Japanese company. She (get up) very early every morning and (leave) the flat before six o'clock. It's not my sort of job!

Last night we (go) to a beer festival. It (be) great fun. You ever (eat) real frankfurters? They're delicious! I (drink) a lot of beer and we (not get home) until after midnight.

Tomorrow I (see) 'Swan Lake' at the ballet and on Wednesday I (go) to Austria for a few days.

I hope everything is going well with you. I (look) forward to staying with you in Oxford next month.

Love,

Lisa

6 WRITING

You are staying with a family in another country. Write a letter to a friend in Britain or the USA. Use the letter above to help you.

PARAGRAPH 1 Say when you left home, and describe the people you are staying with.

PARAGRAPH 2 Describe your stay so far.

PARAGRAPH 3 Say what your future plans are.

PARAGRAPH 4 End your letter.

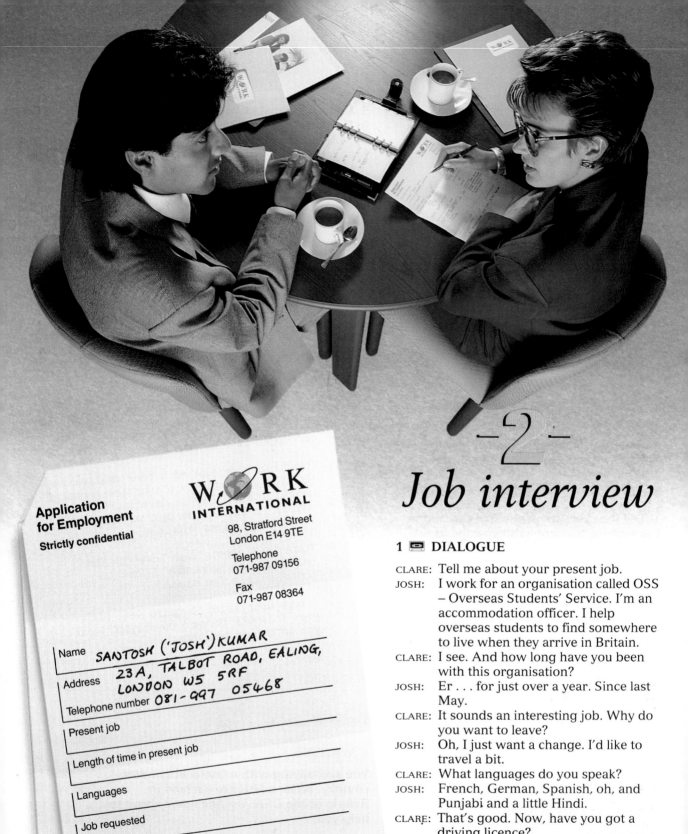

Job interview

Application for Employment
Strictly confidential

W RK INTERNATIONAL

98, Stratford Street
London E14 9TE

Telephone
071-987 09156

Fax
071-987 08364

Name	SANTOSH ('JOSH') KUMAR
Address	23A, TALBOT ROAD, EALING, LONDON W5 5RF
Telephone number	081-997 05468
Present job	
Length of time in present job	
Languages	
Job requested	
Driving Licence	

NO ☐   YES ☐ Time held

1 ▣ DIALOGUE

CLARE: Tell me about your present job.

JOSH: I work for an organisation called OSS – Overseas Students' Service. I'm an accommodation officer. I help overseas students to find somewhere to live when they arrive in Britain.

CLARE: I see. And how long have you been with this organisation?

JOSH: Er . . . for just over a year. Since last May.

CLARE: It sounds an interesting job. Why do you want to leave?

JOSH: Oh, I just want a change. I'd like to travel a bit.

CLARE: What languages do you speak?

JOSH: French, German, Spanish, oh, and Punjabi and a little Hindi.

CLARE: That's good. Now, have you got a driving licence?

JOSH: Yes, I've had one for three years.

CLARE: And what sort of job are you looking for?

JOSH: I'd like a job as a tour guide.

Listen to the dialogue and complete the information on the form.

2 In pairs, make conversations using the prompts below.

A: Where do you live?
B: In (Milan).
A: How long have you lived there?
B: I've lived there for (five) years/since (1988).

1	2
Where do you live?	live there?
Where do you work/study?	be there?
Have you got a car/moped/ bike/pet?	have it?
Have you got a boy/girlfriend? husband/wife?	know him/her? be married?
Have you got a driving licence?	have it?

GRAMMAR FOCUS: Present perfect simple with *for* and *since*

The present perfect tense can be used to talk about events which started in the past and which are not yet finished.

1 I've worked there **for a year**.
2 I've worked there **since last May**.

Which phrase refers to a length of time and which refers to a point of time?

Note
You can sometimes omit *for* in everyday conversation, e.g. *He has been there (for) a week*. You can never omit *since*.

For or since?
1 I've been here . . . an hour.
2 They've lived here . . . 1990.
3 He's worked for me . . . last January.
4 I haven't eaten . . . lunchtime.
5 She's known him . . . two years.

What's the difference in meaning?
1 I've worked there for a year.
2 I worked there for a year.

---

3 ▣ SPEECHWORK

Which three words are stressed in each sentence?

How long have you lived here? How long have you worked there? How long has she had it? How long have they known her? How long has he been here?

Now listen and repeat the phrases. Were you right about the stress?

4 WRITING

Larissa Severo, from Brazil, is interested in a job in Scotland. Use her notes to complete her letter of application.

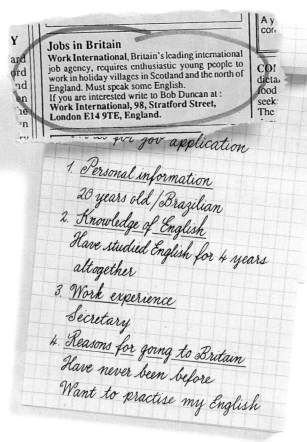

Jobs in Britain
Work International, Britain's leading international job agency, requires enthusiastic young people to work in holiday villages in Scotland and the north of England. Must speak some English.
If you are interested write to Bob Duncan at: Work International, 98, Stratford Street, London E14 9TE, England.

. . . . for you application
1. *Personal information*
   20 years old / Brazilian
2. *Knowledge of English*
   Have studied English for 4 years altogether
3. *Work experience*
   Secretary
4. *Reasons for going to Britain*
   Have never been before
   Want to practise my English

Rua 13° de Maio, 1878/37,
CEP 01327,
São Paulo,
Brazil

Mr Bob Duncan,
Work International,
98, Stratford Street,
London E14 9TE

Dear Mr Duncan,
I would like to apply for a job in a holiday village in Scotland as advertised in 'The Independent'. I am [1] . . . and I come . . . I have [2] . . .

For the last two years I [3] . . . as . . .
I study English in the evenings after work.

I would like to work in Scotland very much because [4] . . .

I look forward to hearing from you.

Yours sincerely,

Larissa Severo

A DAY IN THE LIFE OF

Takashi Takashimi

Takashi Takashimi, a fashion designer from Tokyo, talks to Margot Townsend

Before you read

In pairs, tell each other about a typical weekday in your life.

1 READING

Read and find out what Takashi's average day is like. Is it very different from yours?

Guess the meaning of the words, then check in your dictionary.

partly   jet lag   bright
fashion show   untidy

Answer the questions about Takashi.

1 Why does he get up late?
2 What colour clothes does he like wearing?
3 What sort of restaurants does he hate going to?
4 Why is his home untidy?
5 Why does he spend his weekends in Tokyo?

2 VOCABULARY

Match the symbols with the household jobs in the box.

the cooking   the shopping
the vacuuming   the laundry
the washing up   the ironing

Number 1 is the shopping.

‘I get up every day at about eleven or twelve o'clock. I get up late partly because I travel a lot and get jet lag but also because I don't like getting up early. I never eat breakfast – I sometimes have a cup of tea. I eat nothing during the day. I just don't feel hungry at all.

I live about eight minutes from the office near Shibuya. I drive to the office every morning in my car – a black BMW. I love driving. I always wear black or navy blue. I sometimes wear a white shirt or T-shirt but no bright colours.

I work from about noon till seven in the evening. I don't mind working late. Before a fashion show I usually work until eleven or twelve at night. I eat out in restaurants about six nights a week. I hate going to new restaurants. I usually go to a few old favourites.

I live with my daughter, who's eighteen. The house is always untidy. She doesn't like cooking or cleaning and nor do I! I spend no time at all in my home – it's not a big part of my life.

I usually stay in Tokyo at the weekend. I don't mind that because I hate making plans. The traffic in Tokyo is terrible but sometimes I just get in my car and drive.

clubs – they're
town. Wonder
to get away fr
The people
ferent bac
different
respect,
culture o
and relax
– there ar
unwritten
wife and te
home – th
times we
I go to
morning
sleep. Y
the snc
bed so
life lik
Free f
not
tha

COMMUNICATION FOCUS

Likes and dislikes	Agreeing	Disagreeing	Note
I like/enjoy cooking.	So do I.	I don't.	It is also possible to
I don't mind cleaning.	Nor do I.	I do.	use **neither** instead
I don't like ironing.	Nor do I.	I do.	of **nor**, e.g. *Neither*
I hate cooking.	So do I.	I don't.	*do I.*

3 ▣ SPEECHWORK

Listen and note the stressed words in these sentences.

So do I.   Nor do I.   I do.
I don't.

Now listen and repeat the sentences.

4 In pairs, ask and answer about the following things. Note your partner's answers.

A: Do you like getting up early?
B: No, I don't.
A: Nor do I./Oh, I do./ Oh, I don't mind it.
B: Do you like wearing bright colours?
A: Yes, I do.
B: So do I./Oh, I don't.

Do you like:
– getting up early?
– wearing bright colours?
– going to new restaurants?
– going away for the weekend?
– cooking?
– cleaning?
– making plans?

5 Tell the class about some of the things you both enjoy or don't like doing.

Both of us enjoy/hate . . .
Neither of us likes . . .

6 Look at the survey showing the percentages of men who do housework. In which country are men most helpful in the house? In which country are they least helpful?

JOBS FOR THE BOYS	FRANCE	SWITZERLAND	WEST GERMANY	ITALY	BRITAIN	SPAIN
Washing up	55%	64%	38%	22%	77%	26%
Shopping	60%	58%	41%	43%	48%	45%
Cleaning	51%	35%	40%	34%	73%	32%
Cooking	40%	51%	21%	25%	47%	15%
Laundry	25%	15%	16%	5%	35%	11%
Ironing	20%	6%	10%	3%	29%	6.5%

7 About you

Does the survey surprise you? What happens in your home? Who does most of the household jobs?

8 ▣ LISTENING

Listen to Heinz from Germany talking about how he and his wife, Erika, share the jobs in the house. Note what jobs each of them does.

9 WRITING

Write about your daily routine, what jobs you do in the house and what you like doing in the evenings and at weekends. Use some of these time phrases to help you.

then   immediately afterwards   before/after (lunch)
in the afternoon/evening   at the weekend

–4–
Leisure habits

1 About you

Do you ever buy magazines?
Which ones do you buy regularly?
Do you buy them once a week or less often?

2 In pairs, ask and answer the questions in the survey. Note your partner's answers.

A: Fernando, how often do you buy magazines?
B: Four or five times a year./Hardly ever.

GENTLEMEN'S QUARTERLY
BRITISH EDITION
SEPTEMBER £2.00

SURVEY OF LEISURE HABITS

Ritz Magazine would like to know more about you – not just your age but your habits and opinions. Please fill in the questionnaire and give your name and address if you like. Thank you for your help.

1. How often do you buy magazines?
Once a week
Once a month
Four or five times a year or less
Hardly ever
Never

2. What sort of magazines do you buy?
Fashion and beauty
Motor
Music
Sports
Home and garden
Cooking
Other

3. How often do you go to the cinema on average?
Twice a week
Once a week
Once a fortnight
Once a month
Hardly ever
Never

4. How often do you go to the theatre?
Once a month or more
Three to six times a year
Less than three times a year
Never

5. How often do you go out to the following places?
Disco/Nightclub / Restaurant / Pub/Bar
Two or three times a week
Two or three times a month
Once a month
Hardly ever
Never

6. How often do you do any of the following activities?
Swim / Keep fit / Run / Play any team sport
Two or three times a week
Once a week
Once a month
Hardly ever
Never

7. How often do you go on holiday?
More than twice a year
Twice a year
Once a year
Less than once a year

Name ....
Address ....
....
....

Private Eye:
Confessions
a Voyeur

What Drives
a Man to Ow
Ferrari?

The Independ
Andreas Whi

Changing Col
Autumn Style

Rugby's Leade

GRAMMAR FOCUS
Expressions of frequency

When you want to say how often you do things, you can either use frequency adverbs, e.g. *occasionally* or adverbial phrases, e.g. *once a week*.

Adverbs	Adverbial phrases	
always	once	a week
usually	twice	a fortnight
often	three times	a month
sometimes	four times	a year
occasionally		
hardly ever		
never		

I **hardly ever** buy Newsweek.
I **occasionally** buy Vogue.
It's **always** very interesting.
I buy Newsweek **once a week**.
Cosmopolitan is on sale **once a month**.

Where do frequency adverbs come in a sentence with a main verb like *buy*?

Where do they come in a sentence with the verb *to be*?

Where do adverbial phrases come?

3 Use the magazine survey to tell the class about your partner's habits.

Fernando buys magazines four or five times a year.
or
Fernando hardly ever buys magazines.

4 ▣ SPEECHWORK

The sound /ʌ/ as in *once, month*.

How do you pronounce these words? Not all of them have the /ʌ/ sound.

just   flood   month   book   once   hot
honey   son   sun   trouble   doesn't   house
could   luck   put   Dutch

Now listen and see if you were right.

Before you read

Collect all the answers to the questions about cinema-going in the survey in Exercise 2 and express them in percentages, e.g. 20% of the class go to the cinema once a week.

5 READING

Read the text about British cinema-going habits and complete the chart below. How do the percentages in your class compare with those in Britain?

Twice a month: %
Once a year:
Never:

ABOUT LEISURE HABITS IN BRITAIN

Going to the cinema

According to a recent survey of British leisure habits, the cinema today attracts only 88 million people a year, compared with 1.4 billion in the 1950s. It is a sad fact for the film industry that only 5% of the population go to the cinema more than twice a month, 11% go only once a year and an astonishing 40% never go to the cinema at all. As for the most popular film heroes, in 1989 it was an all male line-up of 1 Indiana Jones, 2 Roger Rabbit, 3 Batman, 4 Tom Cruise in *Rainman* and 5 James Bond.

6 About you

Which do you do more frequently, watch a video or go to the cinema? Which do you prefer?
What have been some of the most popular films in your country in the last few years?

Have you got 'Crocodile Dundee'?

mental Treasure

-5-
Oxford

Oxford is the most popular tourist attraction in Britain, after London and Stratford-upon-Avon. Oxford is famous for its university, which is the oldest in Britain and the third oldest in Europe.

The university has thirty-five separate colleges. For many years, only five of these colleges were for women. However, since 1979 nearly all the colleges have accepted both men and women.

Oxford is not only a university city, it is also a market town, where ordinary people live and work. With over one million visitors a year, it is very difficult nowadays for the residents of Oxford to live their daily lives. Sometimes they feel that the city does not belong to them.

Simon Perrin is a second year undergraduate at Merton College, which is one of the oldest Oxford colleges. It was founded in 1264.
'Oxford is a great place to be as an undergraduate but sometimes you feel as if you are in a goldfish bowl. Everybody wants to see what Oxford students look like and how they live!'

Isabel Santos from Brazil is a student at a language school in North Oxford, where she is studying for her FCE.
'I like Oxford. There is so much history here. The buildings and the river are beautiful. There is everything here – good shops, restaurants and cinemas. In fact, I think Oxford is more fun than London.'

Louisa Williams, who is a nurse, came to Oxford a year ago.
'I'm having a great time here. There are parties every night if you want to go to them. The trouble is, I'm working on night duty at the moment!'

Jack Peters, who works in a car factory in Cowley, a suburb of Oxford, has lived in Oxford for twenty years.
'Oxford has changed a lot. There weren't so many tourists in the 1960s and 1970s. The city was quite pleasant then. But now in the summer it's dreadful. There are cars and people everywhere and hundreds of tourists. Oxford isn't the same any more.'

Glossary
undergraduate A student who is doing a university course for a first degree.

FCE The First Certificate in English examination.

GRAMMAR FOCUS

Non-defining relative clauses with *who*, *which* and *where*

A non-defining relative clause adds more information to that in the main clause.

Louisa, ***who is a nurse***, came to Oxford a year ago.

Merton College, ***which was founded in 1264***, is one of the oldest Oxford colleges.

Isabel is at a language school, ***where she is studying for her FCE***.

Note

If the relative clause is in the middle of a sentence, there are usually commas round it. If it is at the end, there is usually a comma before it.

Before you read

Do you know where Oxford is?
Why is it famous?
Have you been there?

1 📼 READING

Read about Oxford and guess the meaning.

separate   nearly   ordinary   resident
goldfish bowl   pleasant   dreadful

Read the text again and then cover it. What can you remember about the university? Give three facts: about its age, the colleges and women students.

What do the four people do? Note if their opinions are positive, negative, or both positive and negative.

2 About you

What's the name of a famous university city in your country?
Would you like to live in a popular university or tourist city? Why?/Why not? Think of some positive and negative points and note them down. The words below may help you.

crowded   dirty   polluted   noisy
beautiful   interesting   lively   fashionable

3 Join the sentences with *who*, *which* or *where*. Sometimes there are several possibilities.

1 Louisa is a nurse in Oxford. She comes from South London.
2 Isabel comes from São Paulo. She has a large family there.
3 Jack lives in Cowley. Cowley is a suburb of Oxford.
4 Isabel is studying at the Butler School of English. It takes students from all over the world.
5 Simon spent last year in Madrid. He learnt how to speak fluent Spanish there.
6 Louisa works at the Radcliffe. The Radcliffe is a large hospital in Oxford.

4 WRITING

Write some sentences about people and places you know using *who*, *which* or *where*.

My brother Paolo, who is an engineer, lives in Turin.

Evelyn Glennie is a remarkable young woman. At the age of 25, she is one of the world's best solo percussionists. Music critics describe her as 'brilliant' and 'breathtaking' but she has never heard any applause. Evelyn Glennie is deaf and lives in a silent world. She can hear nothing except a few very high sounds.

Evelyn, who has been deaf since she was a young girl, first realised she couldn't hear very well at the age of eight. She was at a piano concert and it was time for her to play her piece. She didn't hear them call her name and a man, who was just behind her, had to tap her on the shoulder to tell her that it was her turn to play.

Over the next few years she became almost completely deaf. In spite of this, she studied piano and percussion at the Royal Academy of Music. She 'hears' by feeling the musical vibrations. 'I can sense musical sound through my body. I hear low sounds in my legs and high sounds in my cheekbones and neck.'

In 1987 Evelyn won the Leonardo da Vinci prize for the best musician of the year. She has already made a record, which has been very

Evelyn can hear high sounds in her cheekbones.

GOOD VIBRATIONS

successful, and she gives concerts about twice a week.

Evelyn has learnt to lip-read perfectly and it is difficult to believe that she is deaf. In fact, Evelyn prefers it that way. She wants to be famous because she is a good musician, not because she has overcome a disability.

Glossary
percussionist A person who plays percussion instruments, e.g. drums, xylophone.

Fluency

UNITS 1-5

1 About you

Do you know any musicians?
Can you or anyone in your family play a
  musical instrument?
What sort of music do you like listening to?

2 ▣ LISTENING

**Listen to three pieces of music and say
which of these instruments you can hear.**

piano   drums   xylophone

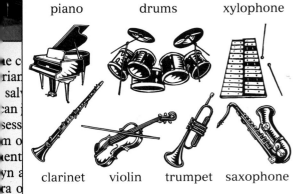

clarinet   violin   trumpet   saxophone

3 READING

**Read about Evelyn Glennie. Find out what
instruments she plays and why she is
unique.**

4 What questions did the interviewer ask
to get the following answers?

1 I'm twenty-five.
2 Since I was a young girl.
3 Nothing except a few very high sounds.
4 When I missed my turn at a concert.
5 At the Royal Academy of Music.
6 Piano and percussion.
7 By feeling the musical vibrations.
8 Yes, I have. In 1987.
9 Twice a week.
10 I try to lip-read.

5 In pairs, use the questions and answers
in Exercise 4 to roleplay the interview
between the reporter and Evelyn Glennie.
Try not to look at your books as you speak.

6 Discuss

Do you know any people who are deaf?
How do they communicate?

7 ROLEPLAY

**In pairs, roleplay the following
conversation.**

STUDENT A	STUDENT B
Ask if Student B likes classical music.	
	Say yes. Say which composers you like best.
Agree or disagree and say who you like.	
	Ask if A has ever been to a concert.
If yes, say when you went and who you saw.	
	Ask if A would like to go to an Evelyn Glennie concert. Explain who she is.
Ask when and where the concert is.	
	Give details.
Say if you would like to go or not.	
	If the answer is yes, arrange a time and place to meet.

Check

1 Write questions using the correct verb tense and the cues in brackets.

Example
1 I live near here. (Which street/live in)
1 Which street do you live in?

1 I live near here. (Which street/live in)
2 This is a good book. (What/read)
3 He's going to get a new car. (What sort/get)
4 She plays tennis quite often. (How often/ play)
5 I come from a large family. (How many brothers and sisters/have/got)
6 We had a wonderful time last night. (Where/go)

2 Rewrite the sentences putting the adverb or adverbial phrase in the correct place.

Example
1 I go to bed before midnight. (hardly ever)
1 I hardly ever go to bed before midnight.

1 I go to bed before midnight. (hardly ever)
2 I go swimming. (once a week)
3 She has marmalade with her cheese. (sometimes)
4 I have Spanish classes. (three times a week)
5 We watch the ten o'clock news. (usually)

3 Complete the parts of these irregular verbs.

Example

| 1 have | . . . | . . . |
| *1 have* | *had* | *had* |

1 have	. . .	. . .
2 go	. . .	. . .
3 come	. . .	. . .
4 bring	. . .	. . .
5 take	. . .	. . .
6 break	. . .	. . .
7 give	. . .	. . .
8 see	. . .	. . .
9 write	. . .	. . .
10 read	. . .	. . .
11 do	. . .	. . .
12 speak	. . .	. . .

4 Answer the questions using a verb in the present perfect simple tense and a time expression with *for* or *since*.

Example
1 How long have you worn glasses? (last year)
1 I've worn glasses since last year.

1 How long have you worn glasses? (last year)
2 How long has he lived in Belgium? (two years)
3 How long have you been in Britain? (three weeks)
4 How long have you had your cat? (1985)
5 How long have you been home? (ten o'clock)

5 Rewrite the sentences choosing between the *ing* form and the infinitive.

Example
1 I enjoy to go/going to new restaurants.
1 I enjoy going to new restaurants.

1 I enjoy to go/going to new restaurants.
2 I want to hear/hearing your new CD.
3 I don't mind to see/seeing the film again.
4 I'd like to phone/phoning the office, if that's all right.
5 I hate to do/doing the washing up.

6 Complete the conversation with *So do I, Nor do I* or *I don't*.

A: What sort of music do you like?
B: I like classical music, opera, that sort of thing.
A: (1) *So do I.* I've got lots of classical records. But I also like modern jazz very much.
B: (2) . . . I find it boring. But my other great interest is sport. Do you like sport?
A: Well, I like volleyball.
B: (3) . . . It's a great game. But I only play about once a month.
A: (4) . . . I don't get a lot of free time now, unfortunately.
B: No, (5) . . . In fact, I'm late for work now. Nice to meet you. Bye!
A: Bye!

7 Join the sentences using a non-defining relative clause starting with *who, which* or *where*.

Example
1 John came to stay last week. He's going to work in Brussels.
1 John, who came to stay last week, is going to work in Brussels.

1 John came to stay last week. He's going to work in Brussels.
2 She spent the morning in the park. She met an old school friend there.
3 Mr Burnham teaches me English. He got married last week.
4 Cambridge University is the second oldest university in Britain. It is about two hours' drive from London.
5 Her middle name is Damaris. It is a Greek name.
6 Carol now lives in Oxford. Her parents also have a house there.

8 Choose the odd word out.

Example
1 washing   cooking   (skiing)   shopping

1 washing   cooking   skiing   shopping
2 come   like   hate   enjoy
3 dirty   polluted   noisy   fashionable
4 always   once   usually   never
5 cinema   concert   theatre   house
6 month   year   midnight   week

CHECK YOUR PROGRESS

Add up your score. How well did you do?

Problem exercises (e.g. *1 Questions, 3 Irregular verbs, . . .*)

LEARNING TO LEARN 1: What sort of student are you?

Here are two types of student. Which one is more like you?

Student A
- You prefer grammar to roleplays and games.
- You don't like making mistakes.
- You prefer working alone.
- You often look words up in your dictionary.

Student B
- You prefer games and activities to grammar.
- You don't mind making mistakes.
- You enjoy being in a group.
- You often don't find time to do homework or learn vocabulary.

If you are more like Student A:
1 Speak as much as possible in class.
2 Don't worry too much about making mistakes.
3 Help others in your class – that way you help yourself to learn.
4 Believe in yourself! You won't always have a dictionary or grammar when you need to speak English.

If you are more like Student B:
1 Try to give more time to learning.
2 Think about what you want to say before you say it.
3 Make sure you understand your mistakes.
4 Try to be more accurate – it's easier for others to understand you!

Preview

UNITS 6–10

💻 **Match the text with the photographs. Then listen and see if you were right.**

A – Excuse me, can you tell me the way to Broad Street, please?
– Yes, of course.

B Lisa's luggage was heavy so she took a taxi to Clare's house in Oxford.

C Lisa,
Here's a spare key. Sorry but I have to leave for work early. Enjoy your first day in Oxford! See you this evening.
Clare

3

4

Lisa

5

D – Are you staying here
long?
– No, I'm going to
Scotland in August.

E – Shall I take these to the
door for you?
– Thanks. And could you
change a £20 note for
me, please?

**In Units 6–10 you will
learn how to:**

– ask for and give
directions
– talk about things you
have to do
– offer to do things
– make requests
– talk about consequences
– describe people and
places

Excuse me, can you tell me the way to the nearest garage?

−6−
Directions

1 About you

Have you ever given or received directions in English? Was it difficult? Why?
Do you usually remember directions?
What sort of landmarks (e.g. a church) are helpful when you give directions?

2 Match the directions with the diagrams.

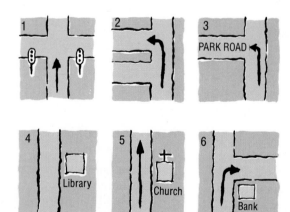

Turn left into Park Road.
Turn right at the bank.
Take the second (turning on the) left.
Go past the church.
Go down/along this road as far as the traffic lights.
The library is on your right.

3 🔊 SPEECHWORK

Which are the stressed words in the two directions below? Listen and check. What sort of words are stressed?

1 Turn left into Church Street and the church is on your right.
2 Take the second right into West Street and turn left at the bank.

Now listen and repeat the directions, making sure you stress the important words.

COMMUNICATION FOCUS

Asking the way
Excuse me, can you tell me the way to the Carlton Hotel?
Excuse me, how do I get to the Carlton Hotel?

Giving directions
Turn right at the bank.
Turn left into Church Street.
Take the second (turning on the) right.
Go past the church.
Go down/along this road as far as the traffic lights.
Go to the end of the road.
The library is on the/your right.

Useful expressions
It's not very far.
It's about a hundred yards/metres.
It's about five minutes' walk.
You can't miss it.

4 Complete the sentences with the missing prepositions. Sometimes there are several possibilities.

1 Turn left . . . the post office.
2 Take the first turning right . . . the High Street.
3 Go . . . this road . . . the cinema.
4 Go . . . the hospital and the church is . . . your right.
5 Can you tell me the way . . . the football stadium?

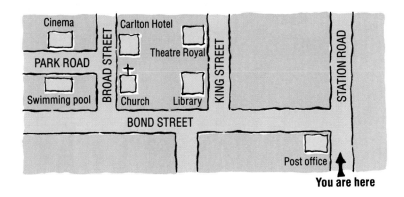

5 Look at the map and complete the dialogue.

MAN: Excuse me, . . . to the Carlton Hotel?
WOMAN: Yes, . . . at the post office into Bond Street. Then take
         . . . into Broad Street. Go . . . Broad Street and the
         hotel is on . . . just . . . the church. You can't miss it.
MAN: Thanks.
WOMAN: You're welcome.

6 Now look at the map again. In pairs, ask for and give directions to the theatre and the swimming pool.

7 🔲 LISTENING

Before you listen

Look at the map of Oxford and find the cross (X) which marks Clare's house.

Listen to the conversation between Clare and Lisa. Follow the directions and mark the place where Lisa wants to go.

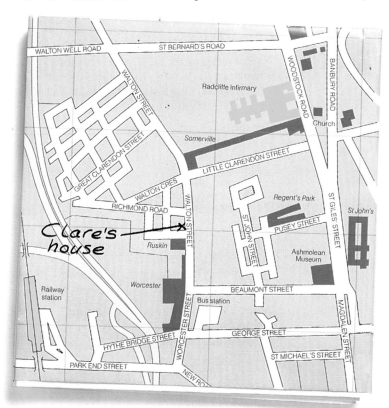

8 Give directions from your home.

Draw a simple map of the area around your home. Mark and label your home and three other places. Exchange maps with your partner. Your partner must now check that you can give directions from your home to these places without looking at the map.

A: How do you get from your house to the station?
B: Turn left outside my house and go along . . .

9 WRITING

Write a note for an English-speaking friend giving directions from either the railway station or bus station to your home.

Dear . . .
This is how you get to my house/flat from the . . .

Hi, beautiful! Are you doing anything this evening?

–7–
Duties

1 🖵 DIALOGUE

Josh has now got a job as a tour guide through Work International. His first job is to take a coach party around Europe.

CLARE: O.K. So is everything all right for Monday?

JOSH: Yes, fine. Oh, just one thing. How much do I have to know about each city?

CLARE: You don't have to be an expert but it helps if you know a little.

JOSH: I see.

CLARE: They use local guides.

JOSH: Ah, that's good. Do things ever go wrong on these trips?

CLARE: Oh, yes, often. You have to be quite resourceful!

Listen and answer the questions.

1 What is Josh's first job?
2 How much does he have to know about each city in Europe?
3 What sort of person does a tour guide have to be?

2 About you

Do you know anyone who has been a tour guide?
Do you think it is an exciting job?

3 Ask and answer about yourselves.

A: What time do you have to be at school for this lesson?
B: I have to be here at half past eight in the morning/evening.

1 What time do you have to be at school/college for this lesson?
2 What jobs do you have to do in your home before you leave in the morning?
3 How many people do you have to buy birthday presents for?
4 Did you have to take a test for this class?

GRAMMAR FOCUS: *Have to*

Have to means that it is necessary or important to do something. The use of *have to* often suggests that someone else is telling you what to do.

Present
I have to meet them at the station.
I don't have to meet them at the airport.

Past
I had to meet them at the station.
I didn't have to meet them at the airport.

Notes
1 *Had to* is the past tense form of *have to*, *have got to* and *must*.
2 *Have to* is often used to talk about routines, e.g. *I have to be at work by 8.30.*

What's the difference in meaning?
1 You mustn't go.
2 You don't have to go.

4 An English-speaking friend is interested in the way you live in your country. In pairs, use the list below to ask and answer about laws in your country.

A: Do you have to carry an ID card all the time?
B: Yes, you do./No, you don't.

Do you have to:
– carry an ID (identity) card all the time?
– show an ID card to buy alcohol?
– do military service if you are a man?
– pay for water?
– pay when you visit the doctor?
– buy your own books at school?
– pay traffic fines on the spot (immediately)?

5 READING

All sorts of things can go wrong

John Byron is a tour guide who takes coach parties through Europe.

All sorts of things can go wrong on these tours. One of the worst problems is when the bookings are wrong. For example, you arrive late at the hotel and there are only thirty beds when you've got forty people on the bus! You have to be very resourceful. You have to sort out problems quickly.
There is always one big drama during a tour. Last year in Austria a man in my party had an asthma attack in the middle of the night and I had to call a doctor. The man couldn't breathe. In fact he nearly died and the hotel owner was very worried because he didn't want a death in his hotel! The doctor forgot to bring any alcohol to sterilise his needles and he had to use some local brandy from the hotel bar! You have to be on your toes all the time in this job! ,

Guess the meaning.

booking   sort out   drama   asthma attack   breathe
sterilise   needle   on your toes

Correct the statements which are wrong.

1 One of the worst problems is arriving late and finding that you are at the wrong hotel.
2 In Austria, a man in John's group nearly died of an asthma attack.
3 The hotel owner was upset because the man was very ill.
4 The doctor forgot his needle.
5 The doctor drank some brandy from the bar.

6 About you

Have you ever had any problems on a school trip, guided tour or package holiday?

7 VOCABULARY

In pairs, choose three adjectives from the box to describe the qualities most needed for each of the jobs below. Use a dictionary for any words you do not know.

1 A teacher has to be . . .

1 a teacher
2 a personal assistant
3 a writer
4 a nurse
5 a model
6 a hairdresser
7 an engineer

reliable   resourceful
patient   efficient
attractive   creative   kind
intelligent   smart
friendly   hardworking
practical

8 🖭 LISTENING

Listen to a manager and note which qualities he thinks are important in a personal assistant. The words in the box in Exercise 7 will help you.

−8−
Polite situations

1 What do you think the people are saying in the picture below?

2 ▣ LISTENING DIALOGUES

Listen and complete the three conversations which match the situations in the picture.

1
BELLBOY: . . . that for you?
WOMAN: . . . That's . . . of you.
BELLBOY: . . . take it to the reception desk.
WOMAN: Thank you very much.

2
WOMAN: . . . borrow your pen?
RECEPTIONIST 1: . . .

3
MAN: . . . some money for me?
RECEPTIONIST 2: . . . How much . . . to change?

COMMUNICATION FOCUS

Offering and giving help
Shall I take that for you?
Can I help you?
I'll take it.

Accepting help
Thank you. That's very kind of you.
Thank you very much.

Refusing help
It's all right, thanks. I can manage.

Making requests
Excuse me, may I borrow your pen?
Can/Could I use your/the phone?
Could you change some money for me?

Agreeing
Yes, of course./Yes, certainly.

Refusing
I'm sorry. I'm afraid I can't.
(Give a reason.)

Notes
Can I/Could I . . . is an informal way of making requests between friends. With strangers it is more polite to use *May I* . . .

3 ▣ SPEECHWORK

Listen and repeat these sentences. Try to make your voice go up at the end. This helps you to sound polite and friendly.

Shall I take that for you?   That's very kind of you.   May I borrow your pen?   Could you change some money for me?

4 You are staying in an international hotel. What would you say in the situations? Work in pairs.

A: May I use the phone?
B: Yes, of course.
A: Thank you.

AT THE RECEPTION DESK
1 Ask if you may use the telephone on the reception desk.
2 Ask the receptionist if you can have a brochure about this week's entertainment.
3 Ask the receptionist if you can have an early morning call tomorrow.

IN YOUR HOTEL ROOM
4 Telephone the reception desk and ask someone to come and turn on the air conditioning.
5 Telephone the reception desk and ask for the international code number for your country.

IN THE HOTEL CORRIDOR
6 An old gentleman cannot open the door to his hotel room. Offer to do it for him.

IN THE HOTEL LIFT
7 You are in the lift with a woman with a young child and lots of luggage. Offer to help.

IN THE HOTEL LOBBY
8 You are waiting for your friend to arrive. The person next to you has just finished reading her newspaper and you would like to borrow it.

5 ROLEPLAY

Student A is in a restaurant in Britain. The restaurant is full. Student B is alone at a table for four. In pairs, roleplay the following conversation.

STUDENT A	STUDENT B
Ask if you may sit at the table.	
	Agree. Say you are waiting for your coffee and that you can't get the waiter's attention.
Offer to call the waiter.	
	Accept the offer.
Call the waiter and ask him to bring B some coffee. Now ask B if you can look at the menu.	
	Give A the menu and ask what A is doing in Britain.

What did they do?

Some visitors from overseas describe their first few days in Britain.

Billy Kwan

from Hong Kong came to study fashion in Coventry. 'I didn't like the food in the student hostel so I spent all my money in Chinese restaurants.'

Luisa Fernandes

from Portugal came to attend a hairdressing convention in Birmingham. 'My luggage didn't arrive so I had to buy a lot of new clothes!'

Inga Johanssen

from Norway came to work as an au pair in North London. 'When I arrived I was very lonely so I joined an international club.'

–9–
Consequences

1 📼 **Listen and read what the people say.**

2 In pairs, ask and answer about the students.

A: Where is Billy from?
B: Hong Kong.
A: Why did he come to Britain?
B: To study fashion.
A: Why did he spend all his money in Chinese restaurants?
B: Because he didn't like the hostel food.

GRAMMAR FOCUS: Conjunctions *because* and *so*

The conjunction *because* introduces a reason:
He joined a club **because he was lonely**. (reason)

The conjunction *so* introduces a consequence:
I was very lonely **so I joined an international club**. (consequence)

---

3 Match the sentences, then join them with *so*.

1 My class was too difficult so I changed classes.

1 My class was too difficult.	I was late for class.
2 I lost my passport.	I had to get a job.
3 I got on the wrong bus.	I took them on a tour of London.
4 All the classes were full.	I visited Ireland.
5 I didn't have much money.	I had to get a new one.
6 It was my parents' first visit to Britain.	I went to another school.
7 I had two weeks' holiday.	I changed classes.

4 📼 **DIALOGUE**

Listen and note down three consequences.

Lisa has come to visit Clare at Work International. She's chatting to Bob over lunch.

LISA: What part of Scotland do you come from?
BOB: Edinburgh. Have you ever been to Scotland?
LISA: No, but I've got plenty of time so I'm planning to go with some friends in August.
BOB: Well, you must see Edinburgh. It's a great city.
LISA: Do you go back there a lot?
BOB: I did at first – about once a month! I felt lonely down here so I went back quite often. But I married an English girl so . . .
LISA: So now you're here for good!
BOB: I hope not!

I hated going to school. There was nobody to explain things; there were no Finnish teachers and no one to teach me Swedish. When the others wrote in Swedish, I wrote in Finnish. The teacher grabbed my pencil and angrily shook his finger at me. I continued to speak and write in Finnish so he called a Finnish boy from a higher class to tell me that writing in Finnish was not allowed.

Soon I began to hate being a Finn so I decided to learn to speak Swedish perfectly. I didn't want anyone to guess that I was not a Swede.

When news came from Finland that my grandmother was dead, I just shrugged my shoulders. But that night I dreamt about Grandma and she called out my name. In the morning I felt homesick so I didn't go to school but lay in bed all day thinking about Finland. I realised that to live happily in Sweden I had to live in conflict with myself. I could never be me.

36

37

Before you read

Have you ever visited a foreign country? Did you enjoy it?

Imagine that you are a child alone in a foreign country and you can't speak a word of the language. How do you think you feel?

5 ▣ READING

Read an extract from a short story by Antti Jalava, a Finn who emigrated from Finland to Sweden as a boy.

6 VOCABULARY

Find a word or expression in the text which has a similar meaning to the following:

1 to tell someone how to do something
2 to take something quickly
3 without making any mistakes
4 to move your shoulders up and down
5 to understand

7 What in the text tells you the following about Antti?

1 It was difficult for Antti to learn Swedish.
2 The teacher didn't like him.
3 He was ashamed of his nationality.
4 He really missed Finland.

8 About you

Do you think it is difficult to 'be yourself' when you speak a foreign language?
Have you ever felt lonely or unhappy in a new and strange situation?

9 WRITING

Write a paragraph about your first day at college, school or work. Say how you felt and what you did.

I remember my first day at . . . I was very nervous/excited because . . .

26

The last great wilderness

A lot of people think that Scotland is a part of England but this is untrue. Scotland is, in fact, a part of Great Britain. It is governed from London but in many ways it is a separate nation. It has its own capital city, Edinburgh, its own laws and its own stamps. It even has its own language, Gaelic, spoken now by only a few people in the islands.

There are only about five million Scots, and most of them live in the southern half of the country called

the 'Lowlands', where the major cities are situated.

But most holiday visitors to Scotland go to the Highlands because of the high mountains and deep valleys, clean rivers and cold 'lochs'. The Highlands are home to many rare birds and animals, like the golden eagle and the wildcat, which are found nowhere else in Britain. It is a lonely, wild and empty land. Only two per cent of the British population live there and the population is getting smaller all the time. There is very little work so most of the young people who are born there have to move south to find a job. Perhaps the Highlands of Scotland will become the last great wilderness of Europe.

A SCOTTISH GLOSSARY

Kilt: A 'skirt' worn by a man.
Tartan: A special criss-cross pattern. There are many different tartan patterns. Each Scottish family or 'clan' has its own tartan, e.g. the Macdonald Tartan.
Scotch whisky: A strong alcoholic drink which gets its special taste from Scotland's fresh highland water.
Harris Tweed: A type of woollen cloth which is made on Harris, an island off the west coast of Scotland.
Bagpipes: The national musical instrument of Scotland which once led Scottish soldiers into battle. Not everyone likes the sound but every town in Scotland has its own bagpipe band.
Robert Burns: The Scottish poet who wrote the famous song 'Auld Lang Syne', which British people sing every New Years' Eve.

-10-
Scotland

1 Before you read

Where is Scotland?
What do you know about it?
What is it famous for?

2 Complete the quiz.

1 What is the capital of Scotland?
   a) Aberdeen   b) Edinburgh   c) Glasgow
2 A tartan kilt is
   a) spotted   b) striped   c) checked
3 A 'loch' is the Scottish word for
   a) a lake   b) a river   c) an island
4 A drink associated with Scotland is
   a) wine   b) lager   c) whisky
5 Bagpipes are a kind of
   a) purse   b) flower   c) musical instrument

3 READING

Read and guess the meaning.

governed   law   major   rare   wild
wilderness

Answer the questions.

1 In what ways is Scotland a separate nation
   from England?
2 Where do most Scots live?
3 Why are the Highlands called 'the last of
   the great wildernesses'?
4 Why are young people moving away from
   the Highlands?

**GRAMMAR FOCUS: Defining relative
clauses with *who*, *which* and *where***

A defining relative clause defines the
person, thing or place we are talking
about.

Tartan is a cloth **which has a special
   criss-cross pattern**.
Robert Burns was a Scottish poet **who
   wrote Auld Lang Syne**.
Harris is an island **where they make
   tweed**.

Note
There is no comma before a defining
relative clause.

---

4 Complete the sentences with *which, who* or *where*.

1 Aviemore is a place in the Scottish
   Highlands . . . people ski.
2 Robert Louis Stevenson was a Scottish
   writer . . . wrote *Dr Jekyll and Mr Hyde*.
3 Gaelic is a language . . . is only spoken by a
   few people.
4 The golden eagle is a rare bird . . . lives in
   the Scottish Highlands.
5 The 'Highlanders' are people . . . live in the
   Scottish Highlands.
6 Harris is the name of the island . . . they
   make Harris tweed.

5 VOCABULARY

**Which is the odd word out? Use a
dictionary if you like.**

1 forest   wood   river   tree
2 lake   sea   ocean   stone
3 valley   mountain   eagle   cliff
4 sea   coast   beach   field
5 flower   rock   bush   plant
6 road   street   stream   path

**Which four words above can you make
into adjectives by adding *y*?**

6 WRITING

**Read about the Lake District in Chile. Is
there a 'lonely, wild and empty place' in
your country? Write a paragraph about it.**

*'The Lake District' area in the south of Chile is
very wild and beautiful. There are many high
mountains, clear lakes and rivers. One of the
most beautiful lakes is called 'Todos Los
Santos'. Behind it is the spectacular volcano,
Osorno, a mountain which is usually covered
in snow.*

Fluency
UNITS 6-10

1 READING

Read the article below about the Edinburgh Festival and answer the questions.

1 When does it take place?
2 What is the 'Fringe'?
3 Where are some fringe events performed?

2 ROLEPLAY

In pairs, roleplay the following conversations.

A telephone conversation

STUDENT A
You have decided to go to the Edinburgh Festival so you ring the Festival Information Centre for some general information. You want to know:
– when the box office is open
– where you can get cheap tickets for the main festival
– where you can buy tickets for the 'Fringe' performances

STUDENT B
You work in the Festival Information Centre. Use the general information leaflet below to give Student A the correct information.

A conversation at the station information office

STUDENT A
You arrive at Waverley railway station in Edinburgh. Go to the information centre on Princes Street and ask for:
– a list of cheap accommodation
– a map of Edinburgh
– the 'Fringe' programme

Ask how much each of them costs. You would also like to leave your luggage. Ask if you can leave it at the information centre while you find a hotel.

STUDENT B
You work in the information centre on Princes Street. Use these notes to answer Student A's requests.

Accommodation list: free

Maps of Edinburgh:
   Small – all sold out
   Large – £1.50

'Fringe' programme: £2.00

NB. People can't leave luggage in the information centre. The left luggage office is in the station next to the newspaper kiosk.

THE EDINBURGH FESTIVAL

If you go to Edinburgh in August, it is difficult to miss the Edinburgh Arts Festival. This is a magnificent event which attracts visitors from all over the world. The unique part of the Edinburgh Festival is the 'Fringe'. This is a programme of events which is not part of the main festival. Many of the 'Fringe' performances are by amateurs. Every year there are approximately nine thousand 'Fringe' events, ranging from jazz concerts to cabaret shows, and from plays to poetry readings. They can take place anywhere – in pubs, churches, school halls, restaurants, old factories – even in car parks!

GENERAL INFORMATION
- Edinburgh International Festival box office: 21, Market Street, Edinburgh, EH1 1BW. Tel: 031 225 5756. Open 10 a.m.–8 p.m. daily.
- Half-price ticket kiosk. Next to the Scottish National Gallery. Open 1 p.m. to 5 p.m. for Main International Festival tickets only.
- Festival Information Centre, National Gallery car park. Open 10 a.m.–6 p.m. daily.
- Fringe box office: 180, High Street, Edinburgh, EH1 1QS. Tel: 031 226 5257.

A conversation in the street

STUDENT A
You have put your luggage in the left luggage office at Waverley Station. Ask Student B for directions to the Cowgate Tourist Hostel. You cannot follow B's directions. Ask him/her to repeat them slowly.

STUDENT B
Use the map of Edinburgh to give Student A directions. When A asks you to repeat the directions, offer to go with A to the hostel. Explain that you are working in a hotel near Cowgate and can easily show A the way.

A conversation with the hostel manager

STUDENT A
You are now at the Cowgate Tourist Hostel. You ask the hostel manager to:
– give you an extra blanket for your room
– book you a ticket for the American-Indian Dance performance

STUDENT B
You are the manager of the Cowgate Tourist Hostel. You always like to keep your guests happy but you cannot book any festival tickets for guests. Tickets are only available from the International Festival box office. Give the guest the address and phone number.

A conversation with a friend

STUDENT A
You meet your friend Student B, who has a job in the Highland Hotel. You are interested in getting a similar job and want to know:
– what time you have to start work
– what sort of jobs you have to do
– how much free time you have

STUDENT B
You have a temporary job in the Highland Hotel. Use the notes below to tell A about your job.

> Start work at 7 a.m.
> Do morning jobs: serve breakfast from 7.30 a.m. – 9.30 a.m.
> Clean the rooms
> Serve morning coffee
> Prepare the vegetables for lunch
> (Free from 12 noon – 6 p.m.)
> Serve dinner from 7 p.m. – 9 p.m.
> Help behind the bar every other day

3 ☐ LISTENING

Listen to Simon, who went to the Edinburgh Festival last year. What happened one evening and what was the consequence?

4 WRITING

You are in Edinburgh. Write a letter to an English-speaking friend.

Tell your friend:
– that you have moved from the Cowgate Tourist Hostel and are now working at the Highland Hotel
– how this happened
– what the job is like
– what festival performances you have seen
– when you are going back home

COWGATE
Tourist Hostel

From as little as £8.00
per night all inclusive

A high quality, indoor…

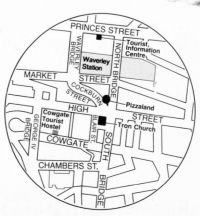

Check

1 Choose the correct word or expression for the conversation.

Example
1 A: Excuse me, can you tell me . . . the
station?
   (a) the way to b) how I must go to
   c) what is the way to

1 A: Excuse me, can you tell me . . . the
station?
   a) the way to b) how I must go to
   c) what is the way to
2 B: Yes, certainly. . . .
   a) Turn to right b) Turn right
   c) Turn the right
3   and then go . . . the church.
   a) past b) along c) at
4   Then . . . the second turning on the left.
   a) go b) take c) walk
   The station is about half way along the
road.
  A: O.K. Thanks. How far is it,
approximately?
5 B: It's about five minutes' . . . from here.
   a) to walk b) walking c) walk
6   You . . . miss it.
   a) don't b) aren't c) can't
  A: Thanks very much.
7 B: . . . welcome!
   a) You're b) You c) Your

2 Complete a female flight attendant's description of her job with the correct form of the verb *have to*.

'With some airlines, female flight attendants
(1) *have to* be young, very attractive and
single. But our airline is different. A female
flight attendant (2) . . . have a friendly
personality and a nice smile but she (3) . . . be
single or very young. Many people prefer an
older attendant. The main thing is to be good
at the job.
   Two weeks ago I (4) . . . fly to the USA
three times in one week. That was hard
work. I (5) . . . look after three young children
on the last flight! Fortunately, I (6) . . . fly
more than once last week.'

3 Complete the sentences about Britain with *mustn't, have to* or *don't have to*.

Example
1 You . . . travel on a bus without a ticket.
1 You mustn't travel on a bus without a ticket.

1 You . . . travel on a bus without a ticket.
2 You . . . take a test to drive a motorcycle.
3 You can vote when you are eighteen but
   you . . . if you don't want to.
4 You . . . cycle at night without lights.
5 You . . . wear a seat belt if you sit in the
   front seat of a car.

4 What do you say?

Example
1 You are in the street. Offer to help an old
lady to cross the road.
1 Shall I help you across the road?

1 You are in the street. Offer to help an old
lady to cross the road.
2 You are having coffee in a friend's house.
Ask if you could have another cup.
3 You are staying in someone's house. Ask if
you may use the telephone.
4 Your friend has left his/her wallet in your
car. Offer to go back and fetch it.
5 You are in a bank. Ask the cashier to
change a £20 note.

5 Match the halves of the sentences, then rewrite them with *so* or *because*.

Example
1 I didn't eat much   b) I wasn't very
                    hungry.
*1 I didn't eat much because I wasn't very
hungry.*

1 I didn't eat much   a) it was too
2 There was no bed   expensive.
3 I went to bed early b) I wasn't very
4 I had a big   hungry.
   breakfast   c) I left early.
5 I didn't buy the   d) I slept on the floor.
   jacket   e) I had to get up at
6 The party wasn't   5 a.m.
   much fun   f) I was very hungry.

6 Write questions for the answers using the words in brackets.

Example
1 He broke his leg last week. (When)
1 When did he break his leg?

1 He broke his leg last week. (When)
2 I won a tennis racquet. (What)
3 She went to work by car. (How)
4 He spent the night at John's house. (Where)
5 I met Kevin in the pub. (Who)
6 He took another week's holiday because he didn't have to go back to work. (Why)

7 Complete the text with the correct past tense form of the verbs in brackets.

A TRUE STORY
It was Cathy's fourteenth birthday. Her mother (1) (make) *made* her a cake and (2) (put) . . . a coin in the cake for good luck. Cathy (3) (eat) . . . the cake but never (4) (find) . . . the coin. Her mother (5) (not notice) . . .

Soon Cathy (6) (become) . . . sick. She couldn't speak. She (7) (go) . . . to hospital but the doctors couldn't find anything wrong with her. For twelve years, Cathy never (8) (speak) . . .

Then one day when she was twenty-six, she (9) (catch) . . . a bad cold and (10) (begin) . . . to cough a lot. Suddenly she (11) (cough) . . . up something small and black – it was the coin! A few days later she (12) (be able) . . . to speak again!

8 Complete the definitions with *who, which* or *where* and the correct word.

Example
1 A person . . . teaches children in a school is a . . .
1 A person who teaches children in a school is a teacher.

1 A person . . . teaches children in a school is a . . .
2 A place . . . you can change money is a . . .
3 A person . . . works in the reception of a hotel is a . . .
4 A piece of land . . . is surrounded by sea is an . . .
5 A person . . . looks after people's hair is a . . .
6 A place . . . you can swim indoors is a . . .
7 An illness . . . affects your breathing is . . .
8 Money . . . you have to pay when you do something wrong is a . . .

9 Rearrange the letters to label each picture.

AMSERT   OFTSER   OMUTNINAS
KELA   HAPT   OWRFLES
SUBH   ORKC   ILEFD

CHECK YOUR PROGRESS

Add up your score. How well did you do?

Problem exercises . . .

LEARNING TO LEARN 2: Using a dictionary

It is important to use a good dictionary when you are learning a language. The best dictionaries will not only tell you what the word means but will also give you a lot of other useful information. For example, it will tell you:

1 How to pronounce a word.
2 What part of speech it is (e.g. noun, verb, adjective).
3 If the word is only used informally.
4 The meaning of the word.
5 An example of the word in a sentence.
6 Any special expressions in which the word is included.

boss /bɒs/
boss /bɒs/ *n*

boss /bɒs/ *n infml*
a person who is in charge of workers
He asked his boss for more money.

You've got to **show them who's boss!**

Preview
UNITS 11-15

🔊 **Match the text with the photographs. Then listen and see if you were right.**

A Many young people in Britain haven't got jobs.

B – Where shall we go this year?
– Why don't we go camping in the south of France?

C We were driving along the road when suddenly the mountain erupted.

D – Have a nice holiday!
– Thanks. I'll send you a postcard.

E And now let's meet the all-woman crew of the boat *Maiden*, which has just completed the Round-the-World yacht race.

In Units 11–15 you will learn how to:

- make predictions and promises
- talk about quantity
- ask for and make suggestions
- ask and talk about completed activities
- talk about past activities

1 Listen and answer *True* or *False*.

1 Bob and his family are going on holiday to France.
2 They are going by train.
3 Mrs Price is going with them.
4 They are going to be away for two weeks.

2 Note down or underline all the uses of *will* ('*ll*) and *won't* in the dialogue.

3 In pairs, one of you is Jane and the other is Mrs Price. Use the notes below to say when you'll do things during your trip to France.

MRS PRICE:	When are you going to buy some petrol?
JANE:	We'll buy some when we get to the motorway.
MRS PRICE:	What about having a snack?
JANE:	We'll have one . . .

Buy some petrol – motorway
Have a snack – Dover
Buy a map of Provence – Calais
Phone home – Calais
Get some new beach towels –
                    camping site

-11-
Predictions and promises

▣ DIALOGUE

MRS PRICE:	Have you got a map of Provence?
JANE:	No, but don't worry. We'll get one in Calais.
MARK:	When are we going, Dad?
BOB:	We won't be long now. Come on, let's go. There'll be a lot of traffic on the M25.
MRS PRICE:	Don't worry about the house. I'll look after it.
JANE:	Thanks, Mum. I'll phone you as soon as we get to France.
MRS PRICE:	Bye! Have a lovely time!
BOB:	Thanks. We'll send you a postcard.
JANE:	Bye, Mum. See you in two weeks.

MEXICO

Acapulco

HOTEL MIRAMAR

- ■ Single and twin-bedded rooms
- ■ Half board: choice of lunch or dinner
- ■ Two minutes from sea

Facilities: swimming pool, bar, restaurant, tennis and all watersports
Bicycle and car hire available
(International driving licence required)

FLIGHTS

Dep. Gatwick Thursday 12.30
Arr. Acapulco 15.30 local time
         (Time difference – 6 hrs)
Coach to resort: 45 minutes approximately

4 ROLEPLAY

In groups of five, one of you is the travel agent (Student A) and the rest of you (Students B, C, D and E) want information about your holiday. Student A uses the travel information to answer the questions.

B: How long will the journey take?
A: It'll take about ten hours altogether.
C: Will we be able to hire a car?
A: Yes, you will.

STUDENT B
how long/journey/take?
what meals/we get in the hotel?

STUDENT C
how/get to the resort from the airport?
be able to hire a car?
need an international driving licence?

STUDENT D
be able to windsurf?
far from hotel to sea?

STUDENT E
be able to rent a moped?
be able to play tennis?

5 In pairs, use the cues to ask for predictions about the future. Respond using *Really? I hope so* or *I hope not*.

A: Who do you think will win the next World Cup?
B: I think (Cameroon) will.
A: Really?

A: When do you think they'll discover a cure for AIDS?
B: I don't know. Maybe in about (two or three years') time.
A: I hope so.

1 Who/win the next World Cup?
2 When/they/discover a cure for AIDS?
3 Who/your next Prime Minister or President/be?
4 What/next year's fashions/be like?
5 Where/you/be in ten years' time?

6 WRITING

Study Bob's note to a business friend.

> MEMO
>
> Dear John,
> I'm afraid I won't be able to come to the meeting on Monday because I'll be away on holiday in France. I'll be back in the office in two weeks' time. I'll phone you as soon as I get back.
> Kind regards,
> Bob.

You are going on holiday tomorrow and won't be able to go to your English classes. Write a note to your teacher explaining why, and telling him/her when you'll be back at school/college. Promise to send a postcard from your holiday resort. Use Bob's note as a model.

Murphy's law of travelling says: 'When you need something urgently, it's always at the bottom of your bag.'

-12-
Quantity (1)

1 READING

Read about Britain's young and homeless and answer the questions.

1 How old are most young people when they leave home?
2 Why do they leave home?
3 What happens after a few months?
4 What happens to the rest of them?

ABOUT THE YOUNG AND HOMELESS IN BRITAIN

Of London's estimated 75,000 homeless people, a high percentage are between the ages of seventeen and twenty-five. Every year in Britain, over 5,000 young people leave home. Most of these young people are over sixteen but some are even younger. Most of them are escaping from an unhappy home life but a few of them just want the bright lights of a big city and a chance to earn some money.

When their money runs out, some start begging or busking to earn money. They start living on the streets and sleeping in doorways or in squats. Many of them return home after a few months but the rest stay. Some say they prefer the freedom of the streets to life at home.

Glossary
a squat An empty building where people live without permission.
busking Playing music in the street to earn money.

2 VOCABULARY

Find a word or expression in the text which has a similar meaning to the following:

1 without somewhere to live
2 an opportunity
3 is all gone
4 asking people for money
5 the entrance to a shop or building
6 being able to do what you want

THE WORLD'S HOMELESS

Homelessness is a worldwide problem.

Australia
25,000 young homeless. Half of them are sleeping on the streets in Sydney.

USA
Washington alone has 20,000 homeless. Only a quarter of them have permanent shelters.

Italy
No government policy for the homeless.

France
At least 20,000 homeless.

Sweden and Japan
Almost no homeless.

The USSR
Says there is no problem with homeless people.

---

3 Read about homeless people in other parts of the world and discuss the questions.

1 Is your country mentioned? If not, do you know how many homeless people there are in your country?
2 Why do you think they are homeless?
3 Where do most of them go?
4 Where do they sleep?
5 How do they get money?

GRAMMAR FOCUS: Quantifiers

Adjectives

All	young people like big cities.
Most	
Many	
Some	
A few	
Both	
No	

Pronouns

All	(of them) like big cities.
Most	
Many	
Some	
A few	
Both	

None (of them) likes big cities.

Note

The following words are all followed by a singular verb: *none, neither, no one/ nobody, everyone/everybody, someone/ somebody, anyone/anybody,* e.g.
*None of us/nobody **likes** big cities.*

4 ▣ SPEECHWORK

Listen and repeat the phrases. Notice that, here, *of* and *them* are weak forms and are pronounced /əv/ and /ðəm/.

all of them   most of them   many of them
some of them   a few of them   none of them

5 In pairs, use the notes below to ask and answer about homeless people, using *all, most, some, a few, none* (*of them*).

A: How many of them have a job when they arrive?
B: None of them.

How many of them:
1 have a job when they arrive? (none)
2 come from poor families? (not all)
3 are under sixteen? (quite a lot)
4 find somewhere to live in the end? (not many)
5 want to find a job? (all)
6 want to live on the streets? (none)

6 ▣ LISTENING

Before you listen

In your dictionary find the meaning of:

an alcoholic   degrading   regret

Listen to part of a radio report about young people who live on the streets and complete the information about Tina.

Name:	. . .
Age:	. . .
Length of time on streets:	. . .
Reason for leaving home:	. . .
Way of earning money:	. . .
Accommodation wanted:	. . .
Job wanted:	. . .
Future ambition:	. . .

7 About you

What do you want to do with your life? Why do you want to learn English? Answer the questions below. Then find out your partner's answers.

A: Are you learning English because you'll be able to get a better job?
B: Yes, I am./Yes, partly./No, not really.

WHY ARE YOU LEARNING ENGLISH?		
Are you learning English because:	You	Partner
1 you'll be able to get a better job?		
2 it is useful when you travel?		
3 you want to go to an English-speaking country?		
4 it will give you a chance to meet new people?		
5 you want to enjoy English literature?		
6 you want to understand the words of pop songs?		
7 you have to learn it at school?		
8 you have an English-speaking boyfriend/girlfriend?		

8 WRITING

Collect the number of *Yes* answers for each question in the questionnaire from the whole class. Then write a paragraph saying why people in your class are learning English.

*All/Most of us are learning English because . . . .
Some of us want to . . . and a few of us . . .*

1

2

Princess

Diana

visits

Hungary

for the

first time

3

nesses.
Britain,
ncess of
m hand
pport to
Hungary.
treasure
famous
his most
not only
elp. With
can busi-
e prince's
unity, who
an branch
velop small
Prince and

| A | Where shall we take her? |

| | Why don't we take her to see the vegetable market? |

| B | We could take her to the Petö Institute.* |

| | That's a good idea. |

| C | What shall we show her? |

| | Let's show her some folk dancing. |

-13-
Suggestions

1 Match the conversations above with the photographs on the left.

2 Some famous people are going to visit your country soon and have decided to come to your school/college/company. Look at the schedule below and in pairs, discuss how to organise the day.

A: Who shall we send to meet them at the airport?

B: Why don't we all go?/Let's all go./We could all go.

11.00 Arrive at airport	Who/send to meet them?
12.00 Visit your school/ company	What/show them?
12.45 Lunch	What/give them to eat?
2.00 Visit famous building	Which one/choose?
3.00 Folk dancing display or traditional entertainment	What sort of dancing/ entertainment/have?
6.30 Reception at your school/company	Where/have it? Who/invite? What present/give them?
7.30 Dinner in town	Where/have it?
9.00 Concert	What sort of concert/ arrange?

*Petö is an institute in Hungary which offers treatment to children with brain damage.

COMMUNICATION FOCUS

Asking for suggestions
What shall I/we do?
Where shall we take her?
Who shall we invite?

Making suggestions
Why don't you/we show her some folk
  dancing?
Why not show her some folk dancing?
We could show her some folk dancing.
Let's show her some folk dancing.

What's the difference in meaning?
1 Where are we going this evening?
2 Where shall we go this evening?

3 ▭ LISTENING DIALOGUE

**Listen and complete the conversation
between Clare and Lisa in the shop.**

CLARE: Which sweater . . . , the green one or
  the brown one?
LISA: . . . both of them.
CLARE: So do I. What . . . ?
LISA: . . . buy them both?
CLARE: No, they're too similar.
LISA: Well, . . . the green one with the
  sheep on it?
CLARE: Yes, O.K. I think you're right.

**Now read your completed dialogue in
pairs.**

**4 In pairs, use the dialogue to discuss
which of the sports items below to buy.**

5 ▭ SPEECHWORK

**Listen to the way *shall I* and *shall we* are
spoken in these examples. Notice how the
sounds are joined together.**

What shall I do? Where shall we sit?

**Now listen and repeat the questions.
Make sure you join the words together.**

What shall I do?   What shall I buy?   What
shall I wear?   Where shall we go?   Where
shall we sit?   When shall we leave?

6 READING

**Read Leo's letter to a magazine and
complete the sentence with the correct
reason.**

Q Leo, 21, from Rotterdam in Holland, writes:

I recently met a Vietnamese girl in my
English class. We have been out together
quite a lot and we like each other very
much. I feel she is the right girl for me. The
trouble is, she lives with her parents and
she doesn't want to take me home
because she thinks that her parents will
disapprove of me. She knows that they
would like her to marry someone from her
own country. Can you help?

Leo is worried because
a) his parents have never liked his
   girlfriends.
b) he thinks his girlfriend's parents won't
   like him.
c) he thinks his girlfriend won't like his
   parents.

7 WRITING

**Write an answer to Leo's letter, giving one
or two suggestions.**

Dear Leo,
*Thank you for your letter. It's not an easy
situation but here are one or two suggestions.
Why don't you . . .*

*I hope my suggestions are helpful. Good luck!
Yours,*
. . .

-14-
Completed activities

Success for Maiden

ON JUNE 28TH 1990, the first all-woman crew to compete in the eight-month Whitbread Round-the-World race arrived in Southampton. The twelve girls, led by 'skipper' Tracy Edwards, completed the 34,000-mile race in their yacht, *Maiden*. They came first in two of the six legs and finished second overall.

Before you read

Have you ever been on a yacht?
Would you like to sail round the world?
Why?/Why not?
What sort of things can go wrong?

FRIDAY 25th JUNE

The wind has just dropped. Everyone is silent and depressed. So far this has been the worst and slowest leg of the race. We still haven't reached the English Channel.

SATURDAY 26th JUNE

At last! We've just passed Land's End. However, with so little wind, we'll probably take two more days to reach Southampton. We're all very hungry. We have already finished all our food. Dawn discovered some emergency rations – chocolate and glucose tablets – so now we're eating those. Nobody has complained yet but I know the girls are feeling quite low. Please God, send us some wind.

MONDAY 28th JUNE 5.30a.m.

We've just come in sight of the Needles. We can see some yachts waiting to welcome us. It feels great but it is sad to think that after so many days we are almost at the end of our journey.

MONDAY 28th JUNE 11.45 a.m.

We've done it! This is the most wonderful day of my life. Now I can rest. I said we could complete the race and we did!

Glossary
skipper (informal) Captain of a ship or yacht.
leg Here, a section of the yacht race.
The Needles A group of white pointed cliffs, a famous landmark for yachts off the south coast of England.

1 READING

Read the extract from Tracy Edwards' log book and correct the sentences.

1 It has suddenly become very windy.
   No, it hasn't. The wind has just dropped.

25th June
1 It has suddenly become very windy.
2 This has been the best and fastest part of the race.
3 They've just entered the English Channel.

26th June
4 They're approaching Land's End.
5 They've got plenty of food.
6 The girls are feeling happy.

28th June
7 They're pleased that the journey is finished.

2 Read and think.

Why did people think Tracy and her crew couldn't complete the race?

3 Read the text again and find sentences with *just, yet, already* and *still*.

GRAMMAR FOCUS
Present perfect simple with *just, already, yet* and *still*

Positive
They've **just** arrived.
They've **already** arrived.

Negative
They haven't arrived **yet**.
They **still** haven't arrived.

Question
Have they arrived **yet**?

Short answer
Yes, they have.
No, they haven't.

What's the position of the adverbs *just, already, still* and *yet* in these sentences?

In what sort of sentences (positive, negative or question) do we use *yet*?

4 Write the adverbs in the correct place in these sentences.

1 We haven't reached the coast of Britain. (yet)
2 We've eaten the emergency rations. (already)
3 We haven't seen any dolphins. (still)
4 Has the New Zealand boat arrived? (yet)
5 The Russians have finished the race. (just)

5 In pairs, take turns to ask if the flights have arrived. The time is 12.25.

A: Has the flight from Geneva arrived yet?
B: Yes, it's already landed.
A: What about the flight from Paris?
B: No, it hasn't arrived yet.

FLIGHT	FROM	EXPECTED	LANDED	REMARKS
SF224	Geneva	1200	1205	Baggage in hall
AF103	Paris	1205		Delayed
PA525	Miami	1210		Delayed
NZ271	Auckland	1210	1215	Baggage in hall
LH534	Munich	1215	1220	Landed
JL895	Tokyo	1220		Delayed
KL454	Amsterdam	1220	1225	Landed
AL238	Rome	1225	1225	Landed

6 LISTENING

Listen and answer *True* or *False*.

1 Eva has already seen the film.
2 Josh saw the film last week.
3 Josh can't pay for the tickets.
4 Eva offers to pay for him.
5 The film starts at 8.10 p.m.

7 ROLEPLAY

In pairs, roleplay a conversation similar to the one between Josh and Eva.

STUDENT A
Ask B if he/she wants/would like to go and see (name of film) with you. Offer to pay if necessary.

STUDENT B
You have already seen the film. You don't mind seeing it again but you haven't any money.

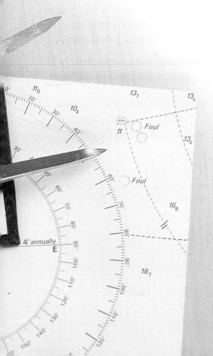

> We stopped for lunch in this little French village yesterday. When we arrived, some old men were playing 'boules' under the trees in the square. It was just like a picture postcard!

-15-
Past activities

GRAMMAR FOCUS: Past continuous

The past continuous describes actions in progress in the past.

In contrast with the past simple
What **were** they **doing** when you arrived?
They **were drinking** coffee outside a café.

At a specific time
What **were** you **doing** at ten o'clock last night?
I **was having** coffee with a friend.

Giving the background to events
We **were camping** in France when forest fires broke out.
While we **were camping** in France, forest fires broke out.

Note
Some verbs are not normally used in the continuous tenses, e.g. *want, like, know*. For a full list see the present continuous section in the Language review.

What's the difference in meaning?
1 What were you doing when you saw the fire?
2 What did you do when you saw the fire?

1 Imagine you visited this village on holiday last year. Look at the scene and say what people in the village were doing when you arrived. Try to make at least ten sentences using the verbs below.

play drink sit talk
write eat look at read
paint

Some old men were playing 'boules'.

2 In pairs, ask what your partner was doing at certain times yesterday.

A: What were you doing at seven o'clock yesterday morning?
B: I was having a shower. What were you doing?
A: I was having breakfast.

1 7 a.m.	5 3 p.m.
2 8.30 a.m.	6 7.30 p.m.
3 11 a.m.	7 9.30 p.m.
4 1 p.m.	8 11 p.m.

43

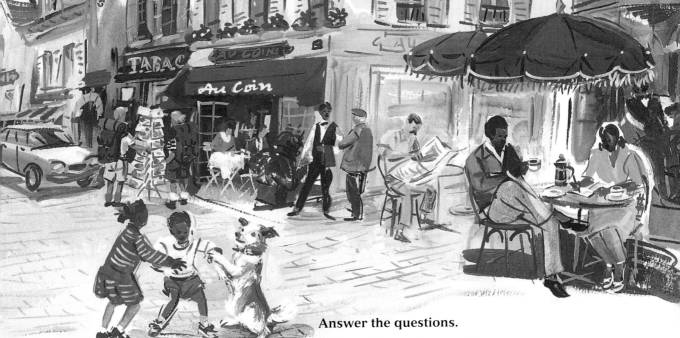

Before you read

Do you have forest fires in your country?
When was the last one?
Was it very serious?

Boats rescue hundreds in forest fires

BY JOHN SHAW IN MARSEILLES

Hundreds of frightened tourists and villagers yesterday escaped France's worst forest fires in twenty years by climbing on to fishing boats.

Flames were spreading along the south-east coast towards Nîmes and Marseilles as people tried to escape.

Many people were wearing only shorts and swimsuits. 'It was like a horror film,' one British holidaymaker said. 'We spent the night on rocks by the sea. There was a lot of smoke. Babies and young children were coughing and crying because they couldn't breathe. In the end a boat rescued us. As we left, our hotel was burning in the distance.'

Last night firefighters were still trying to put out the fires, which have already destroyed 62,000 acres (25,000 hectares) in this region of France during the past three days.

3 READING

Read and guess the meaning.

flame   spread   rescue   burn
in the distance   put out   destroy

Answer the questions.

1 How did people escape?
2 What were many people wearing?
3 Where were they waiting when the boats arrived?
4 Why were the babies and children coughing and crying?
5 What did they see in the distance?

4 🔲 LISTENING

Now listen to a news report of the same incident and answer the questions.

1 Where were the woman and her family staying?
2 What were they doing when the police told them to leave?
3 How did she and her husband help the children?

5 WRITING

Imagine you were camping outside Marseilles in the south-east of France. Write a letter to a friend explaining what happened and why you are coming home early.

PARAGRAPH 1
Say where you were staying and what you were doing at the time of the fires.

PARAGRAPH 2
Say how you escaped.

PARAGRAPH 3
Say what your plans are now.

Start like this:

Dear . . .,
I expect you have heard about the terrible fires in south-east France. Well, we were there! We were . . .

Fluency

UNITS 11-15

1 About you

Have you ever seen dolphins at sea?
If so, what were you doing when
  you saw them?
What were the dolphins doing?

2 READING

**Read the text about dolphins and
put the sentences in the correct order.
Start with C.**

A Suddenly he saw a shark.
B Adam recovered in hospital.
C One day Adam Maguire was surfing
  near Sydney, Australia.
D He was waiting for a large wave.
E He reached the shore.
F The shark attacked him.
G Some dolphins arrived and saved Adam.

3 ROLEPLAY

STUDENT A
You are one of Adam's friends. You were
surfing with Adam when the shark
attacked him. Tell the TV reporter about
the incident.

STUDENT B
You are a TV reporter. Interview Adam's
friend about the shark attack. Use the
question cues below to help you.

When/incident happen?
What/Adam doing at the time?
What/shark do?
Where/the dolphins at the time?
How/they help?
What happened/Adam?

4 🖭 LISTENING

Before you listen

Find the meaning of the words *current* and
push in your dictionary. What is the opposite
of *push*? Why can currents be dangerous
when you are swimming?

You are going to listen to another story
about how a dolphin saved someone's life.
What do you think happened? Suggest your
version of the story.

Now listen and see if you were right.

*BETTY PUTTICK tells us
fascinating true stories of how
these wonderful creatures
have saved lives*

Everybody loves dolphins. Perhaps it's their
smile and their playful personality which
is so appealing. Dolphins are also very
intelligent. Some scientists say that they are
more intelligent than humans. There are many
people who are alive today because dolphins

DOLPHINS

helped them when they were in danger. It is as
if the dolphins have some special telepathic
power.

Teenager Adam Maguire owes his life to a
school of dolphins who came to his aid one
afternoon in February 1989. He was surfing
near Sydney, Australia. He was quite near the
beach but, while he was waiting for the next
big wave, he saw a three-metre-long Great
White shark swimming towards him. Adam
was terrified when the shark took a huge bite
out of his surfboard. The shark then attacked
Adam and bit him. As soon as the shark tasted
Adam's blood, it was clear that it was going to
kill him.

Luckily some dolphins were playing in the
area. The dolphins quickly swam around
Adam in circles. As they did so, they leapt and
splashed in the water and frightened the shark
away. Adam, who was still losing a lot of
blood, managed to swim to the beach. He
went to hospital, where he had an emergency
operation. He recovered and is now able to
walk — thanks to the help of the dolphins.

THE RESCUE

5 Discussion: Dolphin Campaign

Your group wants to raise money to protect dolphins. In groups, discuss which would be the best fund-raising activities.

SELLING PRINTED T-SHIRTS AND PRINTED BADGES

Points to discuss:
- where to get the T-shirts, etc.
- how many to buy
- how much to pay for them
- what slogan to print on them
- where to sell them
- how much to charge for them
- any other suggestions

HAVING A SALE OF SECOND-HAND BOOKS AND CLOTHES

Points to discuss:
- when and where to have the sale
- how to advertise it
- how to collect items to sell
- how much to charge for each item
- any other suggestions

ORGANISING A SPECIAL EVENT LIKE A BARBECUE, PICNIC OR DISCO

Points to discuss:
- which event to organise
- when and where to have it
- who to invite
- how much to charge
- how to sell the tickets
- what food and drink to have
- what sort of music to have
- any other suggestions

Check

1 Complete the conversation with *'ll, will* or *won't*.

A: Thanks for your invitation for Saturday.
B: Oh, (1) *will* you be able to come?
A: Yes, I'm looking forward to it. How many people are coming?
B: I think there (2) . . . be about fifty altogether.
A: Fifty is a lot of people. How are you going to feed so many?
B: Oh, there (3) . . . . be much food. Just a few snacks.
A: (4) . . . you have enough glasses?
B: Don't worry. I (5) . . . hire some more when I buy the drink.
A: O.K. See you on Saturday then.
B: Oh, by the way, is Malcolm coming?
A: I don't know. I (6) . . . phone him and ask.
B: Thanks. Bye!

2 Make responses using the cues in brackets.

Example
1 There's someone on the phone who wants to speak to your mother. (call her)
1 *I'll call her.*

1 There's someone on the phone who wants to speak to your mother. (call her)
2 I haven't got any money. (pay for it)
3 Don't forget to write. (send/postcard)
4 I'm frightened. (be all right)
5 I can't carry it. (carry/for you)
6 When will I get my ticket? (when arrive/airport)

3 Write questions for the answers using the words in brackets and *shall we*.

Example
1 Let's take them to see the Houses of Parliament. (What)
1 *What shall we take them to see?*

1 Let's take them to see the Houses of Parliament. (What)
2 Why don't we sit over there? (Where)
3 Why not invite all of them? (Who)
4 Let's put it in the sitting room. (Where)
5 Why don't we cut it into ten pieces? (How)
6 Why not get them both? (Which one)

4 Read the example conversation. Then write a similar one, using the cues.

Example
A: What shall I wear tonight?
B: Why don't you wear your black jacket?
A: O.K. What shall I wear with it?
B: Why not wear your black boots?

A: make for supper this evening?
B: make Italian risotto?
A: vegetables/have?
B: have tomato salad?

5 Look at the survey of likes and dislikes concerning food. Make six sentences begining with:

everybody   most of them   a lot of them
some of them   not many of them
very few of them   nobody

Food	A	B	C	D	E	F	G	H	I	J
potatoes	✔	✔	✔	✔	✔	✔	✔	✔	✔	✔
turnips	✗	✗	✔	✗	✗	✗	✗	✔	✗	✗
chicken	✔	✔	✔	✗	✔	✔	✔	✔	✗	✔
fish	✔	✗	✗	✔	✗	✗	✔	✔	✗	✗
liver	✗	✗	✗	✗	✗	✗	✗	✗	✗	✗
carrots	✔	✔	✗	✔	✗	✔	✗	✔	✗	✗
salad	✗	✔	✔	✗	✗	✔	✔	✔	✔	✔
People interviewed A–J			Likes ✔				Dislikes ✗			

Examples
1 *Everybody likes potatoes.*
2 *Most of them like . . .*

6 Write answers using *just* or *already* and the present perfect tense.

Example
1 Why don't you read the newspaper? (already)
1 *I've already read it.*

1 Why don't you read the newspaper? (already)
2 Don't forget to phone Clare. (just)
3 Can you return the books to the library? (already)
4 Shall I make the bed? (already)
5 Have a cup of tea! (just)

7 Write the sentences choosing the correct form of the verb.

Example
1 Have you seen/Did you see the new Bruce Willis film yet?
1 Have you seen the new Bruce Willis film yet?

1 Have you seen/Did you see the new Bruce Willis film yet?
2 Which film did you see/have you seen last night?
3 Did you ever ride/Have you ever ridden a mountain bike?
4 When have you been/did you go to the USA?
5 I didn't have/haven't had a holiday this year yet.

8 Rewrite the sentences with the correct tense of the verbs in brackets, past simple or past continuous.

Example
1 While I (drive) along the road, a cat (run) out in front of the car.
1 While I was driving along the road, a cat ran out in front of the car.

1 While I (drive) along the road, a cat (run) out in front of the car.
2 He (break) his leg when he (fall) down the stairs.
3 She (hurt) her ankle while she (play) tennis.
4 While I (have) a bath, the telephone (ring).
5 The man (steal) my handbag when I (not look).
6 When I (sit) down, the chair (break).

9 VOCABULARY

Complete the sentences with the correct word. The number of letters in each word is given in brackets.

1 People work to e . . . money. (4)
People work to earn money.
2 Careful. The soup is very hot. Don't b . . . your mouth. (4)
3 The Whitbread is the name of a yacht r . . . (4)
4 You can't sail when there is no w . . . (4)
5 It is going to be another two days before they r . . . land. (5)
6 You use a t . . . to dry yourself. (5)
7 We didn't want a big lunch so we just had a s . . . (5)
8 Unfortunately we've got no food left and we've also r . . . o . . . of water. (3,3)
9 The fire fighters managed to r . . . the baby from the building. (6)
10 They were late because it was rush hour and there was a lot of t . . . (7)
11 Young people enjoy the f . . . of being able to do what they like. (7)
12 You've got plenty of food so don't c . . . ! (8)
13 You always see lots of c . . . boxes outside supermarkets. (9)
14 Her parents d . . . of her boyfriend so she can't invite him home (10).
15 She would like the o . . . to travel in her job. (11)

CHECK YOUR PROGRESS

Add up your score. How well did you do?

Problem exercises . . .

LEARNING TO LEARN 3: Speaking

Most people learn a language because they want to be able to speak it as fluently as possible. The most successful students are usually those who try to speak as often as possible in class. Here are some ways of improving your fluency:

1 When you hear a new word or structure, say it a few times to yourself before writing it down.
2 Practise reading dialogues aloud when you are on your own. Try shouting or whispering the lines for a change.
3 Always change parts after doing a pair-work exercise. This gives both of you a chance to ask and answer the questions.
4 Practise a roleplay several times, not just once.
5 Don't worry too much about grammar mistakes during discussion or conversation. People are more interested in what you say not how you say it.

Preview
UNITS 16–20

1 Warning: The next pocket he picks might be yours!

Watch out...
There's a thief about!

2
UNDER ~~16~~

WE CAN'T SELL CIGARETTES
TO UNDER 16s.

5

💻 Match the text with the photographs. Then listen and see if you were right.

A	Van Gogh was only thirty-seven when he died.

B	Be careful of pickpockets.

C	There aren't enough trains during the rush hour.

49

3 YOU ARE ADVISED TO **WEAR A SEAT BELT IN THE BACK**

In Units 16–20 you will learn how to:

- talk about quantity
- give advice
- talk about rules
- give warnings
- talk about the lives of famous people

D You aren't allowed to buy cigarettes if you are under sixteen.

E You should wear a seat belt even if you are sitting in the back seat.

-16-
Quantity (2)

Before you listen

What is 'famine'?
Where does it occur in the world? Why?
Does it ever occur in your country?

🔲 DIALOGUE

BOB: Aah, it's nice to be back! What's on TV this evening?

JANE: There's a documentary about famine.

BOB: Another one!

JANE: Bob! How can you say that?

BOB: Well, in my opinion, there are too many programmes on famine and not enough action.

JANE: What do you mean: 'not enough action'?

BOB: Look, the situation has been the same for years now. There still isn't enough food in Africa but there's plenty in the rest of the world. In fact, there's too much in some countries.

JANE: O.K. So what do you suggest?

1 Listen and choose the right answer.

1 There is a documentary programme on TV about
   a) wildlife in Africa.
   b) holidays in Africa.
   c) food shortage in Africa.

2 Bob
   a) wants to watch the documentary.
   b) has seen the documentary before.
   c) has seen documentaries on the same subject before.

3 Jane
   a) is annoyed with Bob.
   b) agrees with Bob.
   c) doesn't hear what Bob said.

4 Bob
   a) thinks there isn't a big problem about famine.
   b) thinks there is too much talk about famine.
   c) thinks the problem of famine has changed recently.

GRAMMAR FOCUS: Quantity words

With countable nouns		With uncountable nouns	
too many		too much	
not many		not much	
a lot (of)	people	a lot (of)	food
plenty (of)		plenty (of)	
(not) enough		(not) enough	

Note

A lot, plenty, too many and too much can be used without a following noun, e.g.
*How many people are there? There are **a lot/plenty/enough/too many**.*
*How much food is there? There's **a lot/plenty/enough/too much**.*

Too much or *too many?*

1 time   2 chairs   3 cars   4 wine
5 work   6 jobs   7 people   8 money

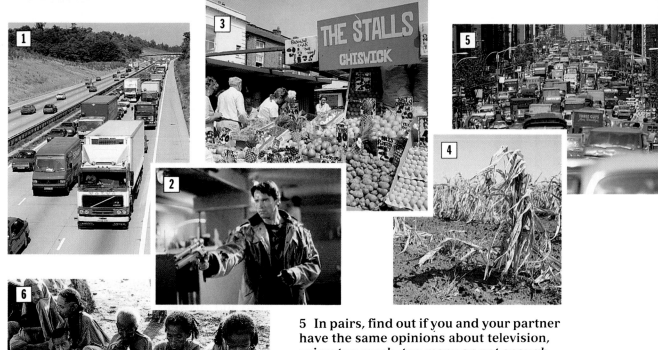

2 Comment on each picture using *too much, too many, not enough* or *plenty of.*

1 There are too many lorries on the roads

1 lorries on the roads
2 violence on TV
3 food in most parts of Europe
4 rain in Africa
5 cars in New York
6 food in Ethiopia

3 About you

Look at the pictures again. Are any of the
situations true of your country?
Is there enough rain and food?
What about traffic in your cities and heavy
lorries on your roads?
What other transport problems are there?

4 ▣ SPEECHWORK

**Which vowel sound is different in each
line?**

1 much   run   can   son
2 lot   hot   note   what
3 many   any   plenty   rainy
4 rough   cough   enough   tough

Now listen and see if you were right.

5 In pairs, find out if you and your partner have the same opinions about television, using *too much, too many* or *not enough.*

Channels	American crime series
Violence	Soap operas
Documentaries	'Chat' shows
Quiz shows	Political programmes
Advertisements	Foreign language films
Sport	. . . (other)
Comedy shows	

A: I think there are too many channels.
B: So do I./I don't. And/But I think there's
   too much violence.
A: Yes, so do I.

6 ▣ LISTENING

**Listen to people from different countries
giving their opinions about television in
their country. Note what they say.**

	Country	Opinion
Speaker 1		
Speaker 2		

7 WRITING

Linking devices

To give an opinion: *In my opinion,* there
aren't enough documentaries.
To emphasise a point: *In fact,* there's too
much violence.
To state a problem: *The trouble is,* most
people like soap operas.
To generalise: *On the whole,* I think that
most of our TV programmes are quite
interesting.

**Write a paragraph giving your opinion of
TV programmes in your country.**

LIVING WITH STRESS

by Roma Marsh

Stress is everywhere in our daily life. And it is not just men who suffer from it but women and young people too.

The main causes of stress are: death, divorce, marriage, money, moving house, changing jobs, ending relationships and taking exams.

So how do you know if you suffer from stress? Do the Stress Test and find out!

STRESS TEST

Do you:	Yes	No
– often sleep badly?	☐	☐
– get headaches a lot?	☐	☐
– find it difficult to relax?	☐	☐
– need alcohol or cigarettes to calm your nerves?	☐	☐
– usually hide your feelings?	☐	☐
– find it difficult to concentrate?	☐	☐
– take tranquillisers or sleeping pills?	☐	☐
– get angry when things go wrong?	☐	☐

If you answer Yes to more than two of these questions, you are one of many people who suffer from stress. So what can you do about it?

Doing yoga or relaxation exercises, chewing gum and playing with worry beads are all common ways of relieving stress. But doctors now say that there are simpler ways. Their advice is that people should laugh and smile more often. When you laugh and smile, your body relaxes. They also say that people – and especially men – ought to cry more frequently. Crying is a natural way of relieving stress.

If you have a special remedy for stress, write to Roma Marsh. If we print your letter, you win £10.

 Next week we look at the problem of insomnia.

-17-
Advice

Before you read

What sort of things cause stress?
What do you do when you feel stressed?

1 READING

Read and answer the questions.

1 What are some common causes of stress?
2 What are some common ways of relieving stress?
3 What simple advice do doctors give?

2 Do the Stress Test in pairs and compare your answers with others in your group or class. Do many people in your group suffer from stress?

COMMUNICATION FOCUS
Advice with *should* and *ought to*

The modal verbs *should* and *ought to* are used to give advice. They both have the same meaning but *ought to* is a little stronger.

Positive
You should laugh more often.
You ought to laugh more often.

Negative
You shouldn't worry so much.
You oughtn't to worry so much.

Question
What should I do?
Should I take a sleeping pill?

GRAMMAR FOCUS
Comparison of adverbs

Most comparative adverbs are formed by adding *more* to the adverb, e.g. *more often, more frequently, more slowly*. However, with short adverbs like *hard, early, late* and *fast*, the comparative is formed by adding *-er*, e.g. *harder, earlier, later*.

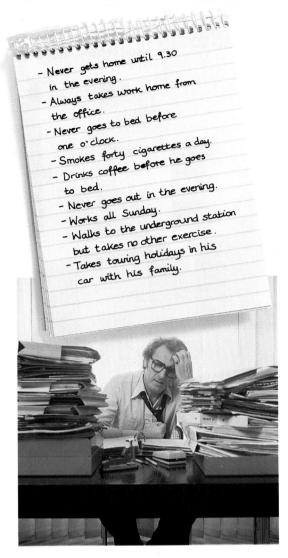

- Never gets home until 9.30 in the evening.
- Always takes work home from the office.
- Never goes to bed before one o'clock.
- Smokes forty cigarettes a day.
- Drinks coffee before he goes to bed.
- Never goes out in the evening.
- Works all Sunday.
- Walks to the underground station but takes no other exercise.
- Takes touring holidays in his car with his family.

3 This man suffers from stress. Look at the notes about his lifestyle. Give advice using *should/ought to* or *shouldn't/ oughtn't to*.

He shouldn't work so late in the evening.
or
He ought to get home earlier.

4 📼 LISTENING

Before you listen

What does *insomnia* mean?
Have you ever taken sleeping pills? How did you feel when you took them?
What sort of things do you usually do before you go to bed?

Now listen to a doctor talking to a patient about insomnia and answer the questions.

1 What should she do during the day?
2 What should she do before she goes to bed?
3 What shouldn't she do?

5 ROLEPLAY

STUDENT A
You notice that your friend B doesn't look very well. Find out what the matter is.

STUDENT B
You are feeling very tired. You can't sleep at night. You've got exams next week and you are working very hard. You usually work until midnight and drink a lot of coffee.

In pairs, roleplay the conversation.

STUDENT A	STUDENT B
Tell Student B he/she doesn't look very well and ask what the matter is.	
	Say you are tired. Say why.
Ask what time B goes to bed.	
	Say when you go to bed.
Give advice. Ask what B usually drinks at night.	
	Say what you drink at night.
Give advice. Ask if B ever takes any exercise.	
	Say what exercise you take.
Give advice.	
	Thank A and say you'll try to do what he/she says.

I won't disturb him now. He's relaxing with his yoga exercises.

I'm afraid you're only allowed to take one piece of hand luggage on the plane.

-18-
Rules

1 Look at the photograph and answer.

Where is Josh?
Who is he talking to?
What is he doing?
What is the problem?

2 Read the instructions below. Say what they mean, using *not allowed to* or *allowed to*.

1 You're not allowed to take more than one piece of hand luggage.

IN THE AIRPORT DEPARTURE HALL
1 No more than one piece of hand luggage.
2 Passengers may check in at any British Airways desk.
3 No passengers beyond this point without a boarding card.

ON THE PLANE
4 No smoking in the toilets.
5 Passengers may smoke in rows 16–20.
6 No pipes or cigars.

COMMUNICATION FOCUS
Permission with *allowed to*

To be allowed to is the passive form of the verb *to allow*. It is used to talk about permission, rules and laws.

Positive (Permission)
You're allowed to take one piece of hand luggage.

Negative (Rules and laws)
You're not allowed to take more than one piece of hand luggage.

Question
Are you allowed to smoke on the plane?

Note
A personal noun/pronoun must always be used, e.g. *Passengers/You are not allowed to smoke in the toilets*. The impersonal pronoun *it* cannot be used with *allowed to*. You cannot say: It is not allowed to smoke in the toilets.

3 💻 SPEECHWORK

The following words all contain the /aʊ/ sound as in *allowed*. Listen and repeat them.

allowed   now   loud   crowd   how
house   brown   out

What are the two spellings used here for the sound /aʊ/?

4 Read about legal ages in Britain.

ABOUT LEGAL AGES IN BRITAIN

These are the legal ages when you are allowed to do things in Britain.

drive a car	17
ride a moped	16
buy cigarettes	16
vote in elections	18
join the army	16
get married with your parents' permission	16
get married without your parents' permission	18

5 In pairs, ask and answer about Britain.

A: When are you allowed to drive a car?
B: (You're allowed to drive a car) when you're seventeen.
A: What about a moped?
B: You're not allowed to ride a moped until you are sixteen.

6 Now ask and answer about your country.

GRAMMAR FOCUS
Adjective + *enough*

He's **old enough** to go into a pub.
He's not **old enough** to buy cigarettes.

Does the word *enough* come before or after the adjective?

7 Make sentences with *not old enough*.

1 He's only three. He's not old enough to go to school.

1 He/three/go to school
2 She/ten/wear make-up
3 He/fifteen/get a job
4 He/sixteen/own a car
5 She/fifty-eight/get a pension

8 What do you think?

Are there any legal ages which you think are silly? Comment on them using *(not) old enough*.

I think it's silly that at sixteen you're old enough to ride a moped but you're not old enough to drive a car.

9 WRITING

Write a short paragraph giving advice to people visiting your country for the first time. Mention any important rules concerning daily life, e.g. clothes when entering churches or sacred buildings, driving and so on.

Clothes
If you are visiting my country you have to remember that you are not allowed to enter churches and cathedrals in beach clothes. In some restaurants, . . .

10 READING

Read about Ranjit, an Indian girl, who talks about growing up in England.

'My parents are devoted Sikhs. They are very strict. I am not allowed to go out at night with either a boy or a girlfriend. That's not because I'm not old enough, it's because of our religion. Eventually my parents will choose a husband for me.'

11 🖸 LISTENING

Now listen to Ranjit and complete the sentences about what she is and isn't allowed to do.

Ranjit is allowed to . . .
She is not allowed to . . . or . . .
She is not allowed either to . . . or to . . . so she is not allowed to . . .

12 About you

Were your parents very strict when you were younger or were you allowed to do what you wanted?
What things were you not allowed to do?
Do you think Ranjit's parents are too strict?
If you go to live in another country, do you think you should follow your original culture and beliefs?

-19-
Warnings

Before you listen

Do you know anything about Amsterdam?
Do many people in your town/capital city
speak English?
Are any parts of your town/capital city
dangerous at night?

**1 Read or listen to Josh's announcement
and answer *True* or *False*.**

1 Most Dutch people speak some English.
2 Tomorrow the tourists are going to a
  Picasso exhibition.
3 They have to give Josh money to buy
  tickets for the exhibition.
4 The visit is in the afternoon.
5 You shouldn't take a lot of money with you
  when you go sightseeing.

📼 READING

Josh is talking to some tourists who have just
arrived in Holland. They are on a coach from
Schipol Airport to the centre of Amsterdam.

'Good morning. My name is Josh Kumar and
I'm your travel guide. Welcome to
Amsterdam. I hope you had a good flight
from Britain.

Now, just a few bits of information for you.
Don't worry if you can't speak Dutch. Almost
everybody speaks some English in
Amsterdam. Most instructions are usually in
four languages, including English!

About tomorrow's programme. Can we
meet outside the hotel at 9.30 a.m. for our
trip to the Van Gogh museum? Please don't
forget to bring your tickets with you.

A word of warning. As in any big city, be
careful of pickpockets. Make sure you don't
take too much money with you when you go
out. Now we are just coming to the Royal
Palace in Dam Square.'

COMMUNICATION FOCUS: Warnings

Give warnings
Be careful of pickpockets.
Watch out/Look out for pickpockets.
Always keep your money safe.
Make sure you keep your money safe.
Never take a lot of money with you.
Don't forget to lock your door.

Accept warnings
Yes, O.K. I will.
It's all right. I'll be careful.
Don't worry. I will./I won't.

2 ▭ SPEECHWORK

Where is the main stress in these warnings?

Watch out!   Look out!   Be careful!

Listen and repeat each warning twice, first quietly and then more loudly.

3 In pairs, use the the notes below to give warnings to visitors in big cities.

A: Never walk/Make sure you don't walk in parks alone after dark.
B: Don't worry, I won't.
A: Always walk/Make sure you walk confidently in the street.
B: Don't worry, I will.

– walk or jog in parks alone after dark
– walk confidently in the street
– put your wallet in your back pocket
– wear expensive jewellery
– fasten your handbag securely
– travel alone on the underground late at night
– sit in an empty compartment

4 VOCABULARY

Complete the missing forms.

ADJECTIVES	ADVERBS
safe	. . .
. . .	securely
confident	. . .
. . .	late
good	. . .
careful	. . .

5 ROLEPLAY

Student A is staying with Student B. A is going out for the evening. Roleplay the situation.

STUDENT A	STUDENT B
Say you are going out for the evening. Say where.	
	Ask when A is going to be back.
Say when.	
	Warn A about coming home alone in the dark and suggest he/she takes a taxi.
Accept suggestion.	
	Warn A about carrying too much money.
Accept warning.	
	Say goodbye. Tell A not to forget his/her key.
Say you won't. Say goodbye.	

6 READING

Read and answer the questions.

1 Who do you think this advice is for?
2 Is it sensible or is it exaggerated?
3 Can you think of any other useful advice?

LOOK CONFIDENT

Muggers like people who look weak and frightened, so walk tall and try to act confidently. If someone asks you the time at night, look them in the eye and say the time–any time–but make sure you don't look down at your watch. If someone asks you for directions, always look at the person when you answer. Don't turn round when you point the way. This may be the chance the mugger is waiting for.

Avoid wearing high heels at night. It is easier to run if you are wearing comfortable shoes. Finally, never be afraid to shout for help or knock on people's doors. ☐

58

─20─
Van Gogh

1 About you

Which famous artists come from your
   country?
Do you have a favourite painting?
Why do you like it?

Before you read

Have you seen any of Van Gogh's paintings?
Do you know anything about his life?
Which painting on this page do you like best?

2 READING

Read about Van Gogh and answer the questions.

1 How many paintings did he sell in his
   lifetime?
2 How old was he when he started painting?
3 What jobs did he have before becoming a
   painter?
4 Where did he paint his most famous
   pictures?
5 What was wrong with him?
6 How did he die?

3 Make questions for the answers.

1 How much are Van Gogh's paintings
   worth today?

1 Millions of pounds.
2 In Holland.
3 In 1886.
4 To a place called Arles in the south of
   France.
5 On Sunday 27th July 1890.

4 VOCABULARY

Which words or phrases in the text tell you the following:

1 what sort of things Van Gogh painted
2 what his paintings are like
3 that he was religious
4 what was wrong with Van Gogh
5 how he killed himself

5 Which words do you think best describe Van Gogh's paintings?

strong   weak   light   dark   energetic
calm   happy   sad   colourful   dull

Which words do you think best describe Van Gogh?

happy   mad   depressed   contented
miserable   creative   boring

Vincent Van Gogh 1853–1890

Nobody has ever painted cornfields or sunflowers like Van
Gogh. His paintings are full
of colour and sunlight. Today his
paintings are worth millions of
pounds but in his lifetime he only sold
one.

Van Gogh was born in Holland
in 1853. He did not start painting
until he was twenty-seven, ten years
before he died. Before becoming a
painter, he was a teacher, an art dealer
and a church preacher.

In 1886 he left Holland and
joined his younger brother, Theo, who
was working in Paris at the time. After
living there for two years, he moved to
the warmer climate of Arles in the
south of France. Here he painted some
of his most famous pictures.

However, Van Gogh was mentally
ill. During one of his fits of madness

6 Look at the Focus box and join these sentences using *before* or *after*.

1 He left Holland. Then he joined his brother, Theo. (After)
2 He arrived in Paris. He made friends with Paul Gauguin. (After)
3 He lived in Paris. Then he moved to Arles. (Before)
4 He spent a year in a mental hospital. Then he shot himself. (After)
5 He said 'La tristesse durera'. Then he died. (Before)

he attacked his friend, the artist Paul Gauguin. In another fit of madness, Van Gogh cut off part of his own ear. Eventually he went into a mental hospital but he did not get any better.

Finally, on Sunday 27th July 1890, in the small village of Auvers, north of Paris, Vincent Van Gogh took a gun, went into a cornfield and shot himself. When his brother Theo arrived, he said: 'I hope I did it properly.' Thirty-six hours later Van Gogh died in his brother's arms. His last words were 'La tristesse durera'. (The sadness will continue.)

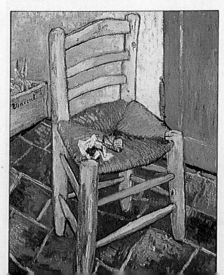

GRAMMAR FOCUS
Time clauses with *after* and *before*

A verb in the *ing* form can be used with *before* and *after* if the subject is the same in both clauses.

Before becoming a painter, Van Gogh was a teacher.
After living in Paris, he moved to Arles.

If the subject is different, a main verb must be used.

Before Van Gogh died, his brother arrived.

Adverb phrases with *during*

During is used with a noun and says *when* something happened, not *how long*.
He died **during** the war. **During** a fit of madness, he cut off part of his ear.

Note
During cannot be used in the same way as *for*. You cannot say: He stayed during three days. You must say: *He stayed **for** three days.*

***During* or *for*?**
1 a month   2 the night   3 the summer
4 a week   5 the holidays   6 a year

7 WRITING

Write some sentences about your past life. Use the notes below to help you.

I left junior/secondary school at the age of . . .
Then I went to . . .
I left . . . in . . .
From 19 . . to 19 . ., I . . .
I am now . . .

Now write a paragraph to link the sentences. Use the words in the box below.

after   (and) then   (two) years later
after that   during the . . .   eventually
finally

After leaving junior/secondary school, I went to . . . Three years later I . . . and . . .

8 What do you think?

Do you think Van Gogh's paintings are worth so much money?

Van Gogh sells for record 51 million

Fluency

UNITS 16–20

1 EMBASSY: an information game for three or four players

You work in the Information Department in your embassy, where your job is to answer questions and give information to people visiting your country. Play the game to see how good you are at the job!

HOW TO PLAY

1 Divide into groups. Each group needs a copy of the questions cut into separate question cards, a dice and a counter for each player.
2 Lay the question cards in a pile, face downwards so that people cannot read them.
3 Each player must throw a six to start and a six to finish.
4 To make a move, throw the dice and move the correct number of squares.
5 If you land on an Embassy-question square, the player on your right takes a question card and asks you the question on the card.
6 If you answer the question satisfactorily, you move on one square. If the other members of your group decide that you have not answered the question well enough, they can ask you to miss a turn.

The winner is the first person to reach the end of the Embassy Working Week.

---

2 WRITING

Write part of an information leaflet for someone visiting your country. Use the answers to five of the questions in the game to help you.

EMBASSY QUESTIONS

Which is the best time of year to visit your country as a tourist? Why?	I am going to visit your country with some teenagers. Are sixteen-year-olds allowed to buy alcoholic drinks?
I want to invite some people to lunch in a restaurant. What is a suitable time to book the table and what restaurant do you recommend?	I would like to spend two weeks driving in your country. Can you tell me about some areas to visit?
I am going to hire a car while I am here. Are there any rules about parking or speed limits in the city?	I would like to visit a university city in your country. Which one is the most famous?
I would like to buy some books about your country. Where is there a good bookshop and how do I get to it?	I come from England. What do people in your country think of the British? Do they like them?
What advice can you give about tipping in taxis, restaurants and hotels?	I am a teacher from the USA. I'm doing some research into schools in other countries. Are there any problems in your schools?
Before entering your country, do I have to get any special documents? If so, what are they and where can I get them?	Have you got any warnings or advice about changing money in your country?
Am I allowed to take my pet dog with me when I go to live in your country?	Can you tell me the names of some beaches where it is clean enough to swim?
Are there any problems about drinking tap water in this country?	What are the rules about riding motorbikes in your country?
I want to see some paintings by some of your country's most famous artists. Where can I go to see them?	Where are the worst areas of pollution in your country?

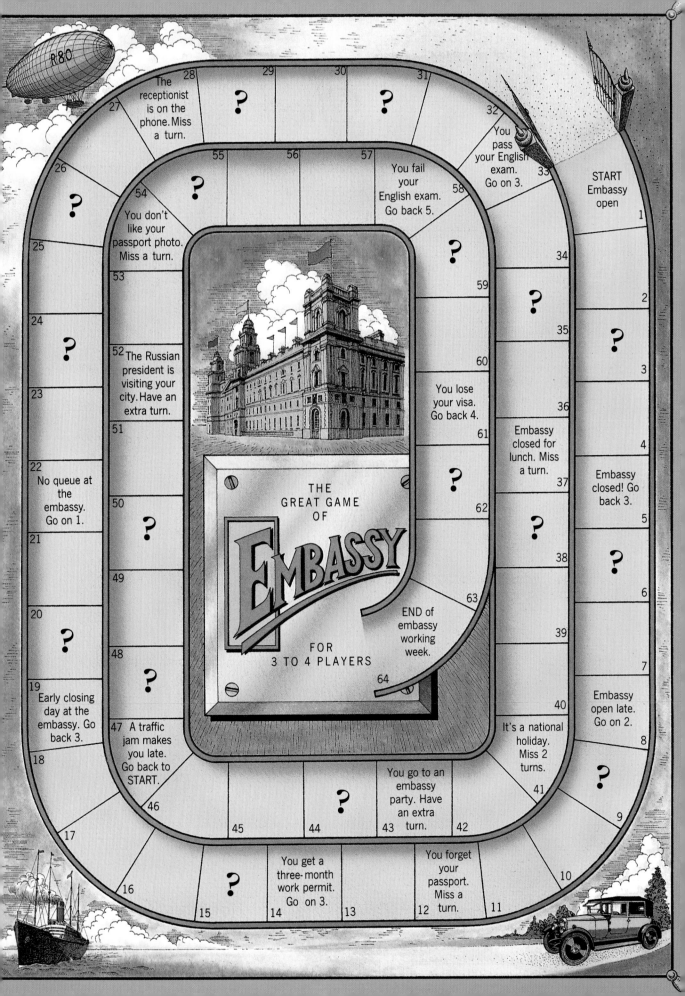

Check

1 Write the words in the correct column.

potatoes books violence sun cars
smoke luggage advertisements
sugar men

TOO MANY	TOO MUCH
potatoes	

2 Complete the sentences using *enough* and one of the following:

smart time old room money well

Example
1 She can't drive yet. She's not . . .
1 She can't drive yet. She's not old enough.

1 She can't drive yet. She's not . . .
2 I want to buy a new pair of jeans but I haven't got . . .
3 We can't have the party in here. There isn't . . .
4 My mother can't come on holiday with us. She isn't . . .
5 I can't wear that old jacket. It isn't . . .
6 They didn't manage to get to the museum. They didn't have . . .

3 Make sensible sentences from the table using *ought to* or *oughtn't to*.

Example
1 You oughtn't to eat so much.

You	ought to oughtn't to	eat so much. take so many sleeping pills. go to bed earlier. drink so much coffee. read more books. smoke so many cigarettes.

4 Match the adverbs with their opposites.

Example
1 c)

1 casually   a) carelessly
2 neatly   b) fast
3 quietly   c) smartly
4 slowly   d) late
5 carefully   e) untidily
6 shyly   f) loudly
7 early   g) confidently

5 Write the comparative form of the adverbs.

Example
1 fast – faster

1 fast   5 quietly
2 often   6 hard
3 early   7 slowly
4 late

6 Rewrite the sentences using *should* and a comparative adverb.

Example
1 He drives too fast.
1 He should drive more slowly.

1 He drives too fast.
2 You go to bed too late.
3 She speaks so fast!
4 You get up too early.
5 They don't go out often enough.
6 He sings so loudly!

7 Make rules for the places or situations.

Example
1 In a library (X) eat or drink
1 You're not allowed to eat or drink in a library.

1 In a library (X) eat or drink
2 In a restaurant (X) wear beach clothes
3 In a petrol station (X) light a cigarette
4 In a theatre (X) smoke
5 On a motorway (X) cycle
6 On a motorway (X) drive over 120 kmph

8 Some young people are staying in your house. Use these sentence openers to tell them what to do while you are away.

Make sure you   Don't forget to
Always   Never

Example
1 Remind them to lock the door when they leave.
1 Don't forget to lock the door when you leave.
2 Warn them not to leave any windows open.
2 Make sure you don't leave any windows open.

1 Remind them to lock the door when they leave.
2 Warn them not to leave any windows open.
3 Tell them always to carry enough money for a taxi.
4 Tell them never to go alone on the underground after midnight.
5 Remind them to water the houseplants.
6 Tell them always to lock the front door when they go to bed.
7 Remind them to feed the cat twice a day.
8 Warn them not to play the radio too loudly.
9 Tell them never to invite strangers into the house.

9 Rewrite any sentences in which you can substitute *before . . . ing* or *after . . . ing*.

Example
1 After I left school, I went to college.
1 After leaving school, I went to college.

1 After I left school, I went to college.
2 After they left, the telephone rang.
3 Before they went out, they had a shower.
4 Before he went to bed, he had a glass of milk.
5 Before Ann took the job, her mother was very worried about her.

10 Complete the text with the correct preposition.

during   for   since   until

My father was born (1) *during* the Second World War. He lived in Barnsley (2) . . . his sixteenth birthday. Then he moved to Birmingham and went to college (3) . . . three years to study engineering. (4) . . . his final year there he met my mother. They have been married (5) . . . 1968 and are still very happy.

CHECK YOUR PROGRESS

Add up your score. How well did you do?

Problem exercises . . .

LEARNING TO LEARN 4: Listening

Many students feel nervous when they are asked to listen to real English on cassette. They worry that they are not going to understand everything, or that the people are going to speak too fast or with strange accents. Here are some useful tips to help you to listen:

1 Relax and don't panic!
2 Use questions in the Students' Book or from your teacher to help you listen for the important information.
3 Don't worry if you don't understand every word. Many British people don't hear every word.
4 Listen in particular for the stressed words. These often contain more information.
5 Remember that listening to real people face-to-face is much easier than listening to a cassette!

Preview

UNITS 21-25

🔲 **Match the text with the photographs. Then listen and see if you were right.**

A – Can I help you?
– Yes, my aunt asked me to pay her newspaper bill. Her name's Clare Taylor: 201, Walton Street.

B – If that's Mr Miller, can you ask him to call me later?
– Yes, O.K.

C – I wonder what the weather will be like this weekend.
– According to the forecast, there may be storms.

D – What's that?
– It's seaweed. It looks a bit strange but it tastes delicious.

E – It's a beautiful garden. You must be keen on gardening.
– I am, but I don't have a lot of time to spend on it.

In Units 21–25 you will learn how to:

– talk about possible events
– make requests and give instructions
– talk about the senses
– draw conclusions
– report requests

-21-
Possibility

Before you listen

Look at the photograph.
Who do you think Clare is talking to?
Where are they?
What time of year is it?
What's the weather like?

🔲 DIALOGUE

ANN: How are things with Lisa?

CLARE: Fine. She's just come back from Scotland. Apparently, they had a heatwave all week!

ANN: That's surprising for Scotland! I think I might give her a ring next week. Perhaps she'd like to have lunch with me one day.

CLARE: I'm sure she'd love to, Mum, but she might not be here. I think she's going to Ireland next week.

ANN: Goodness! When is she going back to Australia?

CLARE: I'm not sure. She may try to get a job here in England for a while. I don't mind. She's no trouble.

ANN: Good. Oh, just look at that sky! I think we're going to have a lovely autumn.

1 Answer *True, False* or *Possibly.*

1 Lisa is in Scotland.
2 The weather has been good in Scotland.
3 Ann is going to telephone Lisa next week.
4 Lisa has plans to go to Ireland next week.
5 She is going to stay longer in Britain.
6 Ann thinks it's going to rain soon.

GRAMMAR FOCUS: *May* and *might*

May and *might* are used to talk about possible future events. In most cases there is no difference in meaning between *may* and *might*.

Positive
I may/might give her a ring.

Negative
She may not/might not be there.

Question	*Short answer*
Are you going to give her a ring?	I may/might. I may/might not.

What's the difference in meaning?
1 I won't be there.   2 I may not be there.

2 In pairs, say why you should take certain things on a walking trip.

A: Shall I take a sweater?
B: Yes, you might get cold.

1 a sweater   4 a pair of binoculars
2 a compass   5 a camera
3 a bar of chocolate   6 some matches

get lost   get hungry   need to light a fire
want to do some birdwatching
want to take some photos   get cold

67

3 In pairs, ask and answer questions about possible future events.

A: Where do you think you'll go for your next holiday?

B: I think I might go to Thailand./I'm going (to go) to Miami Beach.

1 Where do you think you'll go for your next holiday?
2 What are you going to do at the weekend?
3 What are you going to do about your English studies after this course?
4 What's the next article of clothing you are going to buy?
5 What's the next film you are going to see?
6 What do you think the weather will be like tomorrow?

Before you read

What sort of winter did you have last year? What about the summer? Is this typical of your country? Have you had any violent storms or floods recently?

4 READING

Read the text and write predictions.

1 The globe may get warmer.

1 The globe
2 Dry tropical regions
3 Wet tropical regions
4 Tropical storms
5 The middle latitudes
6 The polar ice

5 VOCABULARY

Find a word or expression in the text which has a similar meaning to the following:

1 bad accident or catastrophe
2 world
3 recorded
4 heavy rains in Asian countries
5 storm in the Western Atlantic with circular wind
6 turn from ice to water

6 ☐ LISTENING

Listen to a member of Greenpeace talking about the possible effects of global warming. Note two things he predicts.

GLOBAL WEATHER: WHAT ON EARTH IS HAPPENING?

By our ecology correspondent

IN THE LAST FEW YEARS the news has been full of stories of hurricanes, floods, droughts and other disasters caused by the weather. Scientists agree that something very serious is happening to the world weather. They now think that in the future:

1 The globe may get warmer.
● *Fact:* the six warmest years on record were in the 1980s.

2 Dry tropical regions may become drier. Wet tropical regions may become wetter.
● *Fact:* there has been a drought in Africa's Sahel region for most of the last twenty years. Monsoons have been extremely heavy in South East Asia in the last few years.

3 Tropical storms may become stronger and more frequent.
● *Fact:* Hurricane Gilbert was one of the most powerful hurricanes in the Western Hemisphere this century. In 1988, winds of over 200 miles per hour hit Venezuela, Mexico, Jamaica and Haiti.

4 The middle latitudes of the world may become warmer and drier.
● *Fact:* the grain-growing areas of the USA and the USSR have recently suffered some of the worst droughts ever recorded.

5 The polar ice may begin to melt.
● *Fact:* an iceberg more than twice the size of Luxembourg broke off Antarctica in the autumn of 1987.

Sea levels may rise by one metre or more.

Requests and instructions

1 ▣ LISTENING DIALOGUE

Listen and complete the dialogue.

CLARE: By the way, someone . . . you last
night. His name was Angus.
LISA: Oh . . . Angus.
CLARE: Who's Angus?
LISA: Oh, just . . . in Scotland last week.
Listen, . . . again, . . .?
CLARE: That's not very kind!
LISA: I don't care. He's very . . .
CLARE: O.K. Well, I'm . . . now. . . . time, . . .
some bread, please?
LISA: O.K. I will. . . . day!
CLARE: And you. Bye!

2 Choose the right answer.

1 Lisa had a phone call last night from
  a) an Australian friend of hers.
  b) a man called Angus.
  c) a friend of Clare's.

2 When she hears about the call, Lisa is
  a) very upset.
  b) not very pleased.
  c) very excited.

3 Lisa
  a) doesn't want to talk to Angus.
  b) tells him not to phone again.
  c) will be out when he phones again.

4 Clare is going
  a) to go to work.
  b) to phone Angus.
  c) to buy some bread.

GRAMMAR FOCUS: *Ask* and *tell* with requests and instructions

When we make requests and give
instructions, *ask* and *tell* are followed by
an object pronoun (or noun) and a verb in
the infinitive.

Positive
(Can you) **ask/tell her to phone** back
later?

Negative
(Could you) **ask/tell her not to phone** me
at work?

Note
Tell must always be followed by an object
or object pronoun. You cannot say: ~~Tell
that I'm out.~~ You must say: *Tell **him** that
I'm out.*

3 In pairs, read the situations and decide on jobs to ask people to do after a party.

A: What shall I ask (Catarina) to do?
B: Can you ask her to wash up the glasses?

1 the glasses are dirty
2 the room smells of smoke
3 there is still food on the table
4 the floor is dirty
5 the ashtrays are full of cigarette ends
6 the furniture is in another room
7 the lights are all on
8 there's a lot of rubbish in the kitchen

COMMUNICATION FOCUS: *If* clauses with requests

If clauses are often used with requests. The verb in the *if* clause is usually in the present simple tense, even though it refers to an action in the future.

If you see John, can/could you tell him to phone me?

4 ◼ SPEECHWORK

Listen to two ways of saying the same sentence. Which do you think sounds more friendly and polite?

If he phones, can you tell him I'm out?

Now repeat these sentences. Try to sound polite each time.

If you're back early, can you buy some bread?
If you have time, could you make lunch?
If he's early, can you give him a cup of tea?
If my mother calls, can you take a message?

5 In pairs, use the cues to complete Clare's instructions to her secretary and make a suitable reply.

A: If Mr Miller arrives early, could you ask him to wait in my office?
B: Yes, I will./Yes, certainly.

1 Mr Miller/arrive/early/ /ask him to wait in my office
2 my office/be/untidy/ /tidy it
3 Mr Miller/get impatient/ /ask Bob to talk to him
4 I/be/very late/ /tell Bob to start the meeting without me
5 you/have time/ /phone Josh Kumar
6 the bank manager/phone/ /ask him to phone back

6 In pairs, make short conversations.

> SITUATION 1
> You are going away for two weeks. You think an important letter is going to arrive while you are away. What do you say to your mother/father/friend?

SITUATION 2
You know that a girl you do not like is going to try and phone you this evening. You do not want to speak to her. Your mother/father/friend is also in the house. What do you say to him/her?

SITUATION 3
Some friends are staying in your house while you are on holiday. You want to make sure they know what to do if something goes wrong. You have a nice neighbour. What do you say to your friends?

7 WRITING

Short expressions with *if*, e.g. *if so, if not, if possible* are quite common, especially in written English, e.g.

Have you got a copy of the latest Tom Wolfe novel? **If so**, *can you send me one? I'd like you to send it at once,* **if possible**. **If not**, *can you order one for me?*

Bob's wife Jane leaves him a message. Complete it with one of the expressions with *if*.

Bob,
Paul phoned. If you're home before six, could you phone him at work on 071-727 6441? ......, could you phone him at home this evening, before 10 p.m. ......? I might be late home because I've got a meeting. ......, could you start making dinner?
Thanks. See you later.
Love,
Jane

70

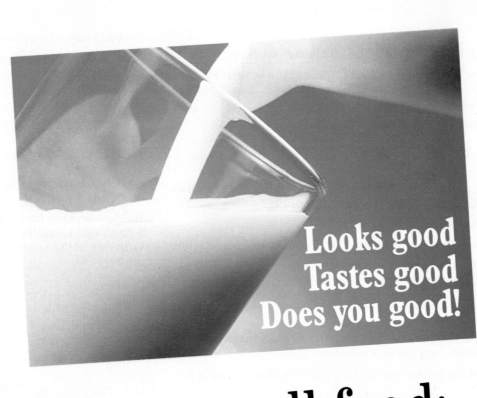

**Looks good
Tastes good
Does you good!**

How to sell food: a question of image

Advertising is about creating images, and this is especially true when advertising food and drink. What the food looks like is more important than what it tastes like.

To sell food successfully, it must look appetizing. Milk must look cold, bread must look freshly-baked, fruit must look ripe and juicy. Television advertising of food often uses movement. Apparently, food looks especially appetizing if it moves. Chocolate sauce looks more delicious when you see it being poured over ice cream than if it is in a jug.

Sound effects – but not background music – also help to sell food: sausages sizzling in a frying pan are mouth-watering.

A TV advertisement for a brand of coffee had the sound of coffee percolating in the background. The advertisement was so successful that it lasted five years.

The colour of food and the colour of packaging is also very important. If the colour of the food looks wrong, people won't eat it because they associate food with certain colours. Nobody would seriously eat blue bread or drink blue beer. Other unpopular food colours are purple, grey and in some cases, white.

How people expect something to taste often influences how it actually does taste. Researchers gave some mineral water to two groups of people. They told one group that the water was

mineral water and asked: 'What does it taste like?' The answer was: 'It tastes nice.' Then the researchers told the other group that the mineral water was tap water. This second group said the water tasted a bit strange and not very nice. The word 'tap' created an unpleasant image of chlorine.

It is the same with packaging. A food manufacturer was trying to decide whether to sell his product in a glass jar or a can. He gave a group of people the same product in both a glass jar and a can, and asked them to taste it. They all claimed that the product in the glass jar tasted better.

So it seems to be true, image is everything.

-23-
The senses

1 READING

Read and guess the meaning.

image appetizing ripe pour sound effect
sizzle percolate associate tap jar claim

2 Choose the right answer.

1 It helps to advertise food if you have
   a) background music.
   b) sound effects of food.
   c) percolating coffee in the background.

2 In an experiment, the people who said
   their water didn't taste nice were tasting
   a) mineral water.
   b) tap water.
   c) chlorinated water.

3 The people in the glass jar and can
   experiment were tasting
   a) the same product.
   b) different products.

GRAMMAR FOCUS: Stative verbs

Adjectives can be used after certain
stative verbs e.g. *sound, look, feel, taste,
smell, seem.* These verbs can also be
combined with *like* to compare things.

Verb + adjective

He sounds nice.	It tastes disgusting.
It feels good.	She seems tired.

Verb + *like*

This music **sounds like** Mozart.
This man **looks like** you.
This room **feels like** home.
This meat **tastes like** chicken.
It **smells like** fish.
It **seems like** a year since I saw you.

Question	Answer
What does it look like?	It looks like meat.
How does it smell?	It smells fishy.

3 In pairs, ask and answer the questions.

A: Why do people often like wearing old
clothes at the weekend?
B: Because they feel comfortable.

1 Why do people often like wearing old
   clothes at the weekend?
2 How does a lemon taste?
3 How do you look when you come back
   from a summer holiday?
4 How does 'onion ice cream' sound to you?
5 How does fresh coffee smell?

4 In pairs, find out if your partner has eaten any of the following:

octopus raw fish caviare sheep's eyes
paella tongue seaweed snake
horse meat brains avocado pear

A: Have you ever eaten octopus?
B: Yes, I have./No, I haven't.
A: What's it like?/What does it taste like?
B: It's nice./It tastes nice./It tastes like fish.

5 In pairs, do the quiz below and find out how sensual you are.

ıce in
ın feel
ıt food
ior the
ıpend
ut it.
ıtable
' the
ıade
g my
·d or
·ould
· into
uldn't

·icult
<, I
ıyself
were
·apa-
much

ap-
nsion
But I
· get
.ll the
·e the
·man-
ed to
aited.

How *Sensual* are you?

❶ Do you have a favourite season?
❷ Do you have favourite smells?
❸ Do you like rainbows?
❹ Do you enjoy tasting new foods?
❺ Do you enjoy beautiful sunsets?
❻ Do you like having a massage?
❼ Do you like touching people you like?
❽ Does music ever make you cry?
❾ Do you like touching certain special fabrics?
❿ Do smells and sounds have special memories for you?

Check your score
7–10: You are a very sensual person. You get great pleasure from beautiful sounds, sights and smells.
3–6: Your senses are quite well developed. You have some very sensual moments.
Less than 3: You are a cool person. Nothing excites you very much and you do not care very much about sensual pleasures.

-24-
Conclusions

1 VOCABULARY

Look at the picture and find the following:

a pipe   a vase   an ashtray   an ornament
a walking stick   a violin
a typewriter   a photograph   a fireplace
a clock   a mask   a bookcase

What else can you see in the picture?

2 Read what the people say about the owner of the room in the picture. Then use these notes and the Focus box to say who you think lives there.

A: Does the room belong to a man or a woman?
B: It must belong to a man.
A: Why?
B: Because there's a pipe on the table.
A: He can't be English.
B: Why not?

1 Sex/nationality/age
2 Status (married/divorced/single?)
3 Family (children?)
4 Location of house (which country?)
5 Interests
6 Occupation (musician/retired?)

COMMUNICATION FOCUS
Drawing conclusions

We use *must, might, could* and *can't* to draw conclusions after given facts.

Drawing definite conclusions
They must be English. (Look at their clothes!)
He can't be Italian. (His name's Juan.)

Drawing possible conclusions
He could be Spanish. (His name's Juan.)
She might be American. (Listen to her accent.)

What's the difference in meaning?
1 He could be married.
2 He can't be married!

It must belong to a man. It doesn't look like a woman's room.

Yes, and he can't be young — there's a walking stick.

Well, I don't know. He might be young and have a bad leg.

3 ▭ SPEECHWORK

Listen and look at the way the /t/ and /d/ sounds at the end of *must, might, can't* and *could* are joined together with the /b/ sound in *be*.

It must be hers.   It can't be his.   It could be yours.   It might be mine.   It can't be ours.

Now listen and repeat the sentences.

4 ▭ LISTENING

Listen to the sounds and look at the suggested explanations. Do you agree? What do you think the sounds are?

1 a car starting up   3 gunfire
2 someone having a shower   4 a baby

A: It can't be . . . It's (too) . . ./. . . doesn't sound like that.
B: It must be . . ., or it could be . . ., I suppose.

5 ROLEPLAY

Students A and B are waiting to meet an English-speaking friend outside a cinema. The film is about to start and their friend has not yet arrived. They know that their friend:

– does not know his/her way round the town very well.
– is going to come to the cinema straight from work.
– has recently been ill.
– is going to drive to the cinema and parking is difficult.

They also know that the same film is showing at another cinema in town.

In pairs, draw some conclusions about why the friend has not yet arrived and decide what to do.

A: I wonder where (Sabina) is.
B: She might be lost. She doesn't know her way round town very well.
A: No, she can't be lost. But she might be . . .

6 WRITING

Imagine that you are the English-speaking friend who didn't turn up at the cinema. Write a note of apology to your friends and explain what happened.

Dear . . .,
I'm sorry I didn't meet you at the cinema last night but . . .

-25-
Reported requests

Before you listen

Would you like a job on the other side of the world?

What are the problems about leaving home for a long time?

▣ DIALOGUE

JOSH: I got a phone call from Clare Taylor today, from Work International.

EVA: What did she want?

JOSH: Apparently there's a vacancy for a tour guide in Venezuela. She wants me to go and see her about it.

EVA: Venezuela! How long for?

JOSH: Six months.

EVA: That's a long time. When does the job start?

JOSH: Well, I haven't decided to take it yet but the travel company would like me to go at the end of September.

EVA: Oh.

JOSH: Anyway, I asked Clare to get a few more details.

1 Listen and answer the questions.

1 What did Clare phone Josh about?
2 Is he going to take it?
3 Does Eva sound excited or upset?

2 ▣ SPEECHWORK

Listen to five short conversations. In each conversation a person says *Oh*. Match the way the person says *Oh* with one of these adjectives.

disappointed frustrated interested
pleased uninterested

Now practise saying *Oh* in the five different ways.

3 Look at these lines from the dialogue. What do you think were the original requests?

1 She wants me to go and see her about it.
2 They'd like me to go at the end of September.
3 I asked Clare to get a few more details.

1 Can you/Could you . . .

GRAMMAR FOCUS
Reported requests and commands

Reported requests and commands are made by using verbs like *want, would like, ask* and *tell* with an object and an infinitive.

Direct (Positive)
'Can you come and see me about the job?' (request)
'Talk to Bob about the job.' (command)

Reported
Clare **asked/wants/would like me to go** and see her about the job.
Clare **told me to talk** to Bob about it.

Direct (Negative)
'Please don't phone me.' (request)
'Don't phone me.' (command)

Reported
Alan **asked/told me not to phone** him.

What's the difference in meaning?
1 He asked me to go.
2 He told me to go.

4 In pairs, ask and answer about the pictures using *want her/him/them to* . . .

A: What does the mother want her daughter to do?

B: She wants her to tidy her room.

1 tidy/room

2 help/cross/road

3 do/shopping

4 fly/Stockholm

5 🔲 LISTENING

Clare telephoned Josh about the job in Venezuela. What were her requests? Listen and complete the sentences.

She asked . . .

She asked . . .

She told . . .

Before you read

What was the last hijacking incident you can remember?
Who was responsible?
What happened?

6 READING

Read and answer the questions.

1 Where and when did the hijacking take place?
2 Where did the plane have to land?
3 Did the passengers get off the plane safely?

Hijack on BA flight

FOR passengers travelling on flight number BA 259 from London to Caracas on Tuesday, the journey which started so well turned into a nightmare.

'It was a terrible ordeal,' says 29-year-old teacher, Emily Davies. 'We were having lunch when suddenly two men with guns and masks appeared in the aisle and told us all to put our hands on our heads. A woman sitting next to me screamed and one of the men told her to shut up. They were really nasty.'

Five minutes earlier hijackers told Captain Horley, the pilot of the British Airways jumbo jet, to fly the plane to the United States.

'It all happened very suddenly. A man came to the cockpit, pushed a gun in my back and told me to fly the plane to Miami. I had very little choice.'

Another passenger on board, a priest, helped to comfort passengers.

'They asked me to say a prayer and I did. It seemed to work.'

At 3.40 p.m. the plane landed in Miami but passengers had to spend ten hours on the plane as hostages before the hijackers surrendered.

'It was a very frightening experience,' says flight attendant Kathy Stewart. 'I hope I never have to go through it again.'

7 Put the following events in the correct order.

The priest said a prayer.
The hijackers surrendered.
The plane took off from Heathrow Airport.
The hijackers told everyone to put their hands on their heads.
The flight attendants served lunch.
The plane landed at Miami airport.
A woman screamed.

8 VOCABULARY

Find words in the text which mean the *opposite* of the following:

1 wonderful
2 disappeared
3 pleasant
4 slowly
5 pull
6 took off
7 to make anxious
8 continued to fight

76

The circles in the corn

By MIKE SINCLAIR

Circles like this have appeared all over the West of England every summer for the past ten years. Farmers have woken up in the morning to find strange, almost perfect circles in the middle of their cornfields. Now all sorts of people are trying to explain how the circles are formed. So far no one has given a satisfactory answer.

The circles vary from two metres to about forty metres in diameter. Experts from all over the world have come to England to examine the most recent circles. The Americans, the Canadians and the Japanese are becoming extremely interested because circles have appeared in their countries as well.

There have been many explanations for the circles. Some people have suggested that the circles are made by tractors (but there are never any marks of tractor wheels). Others think that they might be the result of helicopters hovering over the cornfields, or even that they could be the marks from alien spaceships. One witness reported that she heard buzzing sounds which 'sounded like helicopters' and saw 'strange little lights' which looked like 'lots of candles'. There has even been a suggestion that the marks come from lovesick hedgehogs running round in circles! On the other hand they may simply be a hoax.

However, scientists are sure that there must be a sensible explanation for the mysterious circles. The most recent theory is that they are the result of sudden whirlwinds caused by a fall in temperature on summer nights. So, as Dr Meaden of the Tornado and Storm Research Organisation says: 'The wind may be the answer but it could be another fifty years before we know exactly how. This means we will probably have another fifty years of spaceship theories to look forward to.' But whatever the scientists say, summer just wouldn't be the same without the circles in the cornfields.

Glossary
a hoax A trick which makes people believe something that isn't true.

Fluency

UNITS 21-25

Before you read

Have circles like the ones in the photograph ever appeared in your country? If so, where and when?
What do you think causes them?

1 READING

Now read the text to see if your explanations are the same.

2 Complete the information.

Phenomenon: crop circles
Size: . . .
Location: . . .
Other locations: . . .
Possible explanations:
  Least sensible: 1 . . .
                     2 . . .
                     3 . . .
                     4 . . .
  Most sensible: 5 . . .
                     6 . . .

3 LISTENING

You are the assistant in the news office. Listen to two messages for Mike Sinclair and use the memo pad to make a note of them.

TELEPHONE MESSAGE

Date:

Time:

Message for:

Message from:

Message

4 ROLEPLAY

STUDENT A
You are an assistant to Mike Sinclair, the newspaper reporter. Answer the phone and follow the cues.

STUDENT B
You are a farmer who lives in the west of England. You have received a message to call Mike Sinclair, the newspaper reporter, at his office.

STUDENT A	STUDENT B
Answer the phone and ask if you can help.	
	Say who you are and who you would like to speak to.
Say that Mr Sinclair is out of the office at the moment.	
	Say that Mr Sinclair asked you to phone him at 2 p.m. Ask where he might be.
Suggest where you think he may be and what time you think he will be back. Ask if you can take a message.	
	Ask the assistant to tell Mr Sinclair to meet you at your farm at 11 a.m. tomorrow.
Confirm this. Ask if there is any other message.	
	Say no.
Say that you'll give Mr Sinclair the message, and say goodbye.	

5 Discuss

Are there any other unexplained mysteries you know about?

Check

1 Choose the correct answer to complete the conversation.

Jenny and Tom have had a party. It has just finished.

Example
JENNY: There's a taxi outside. Whose is it?
TOM: I'm not sure. I think it (1) . . . be
John's. He was telephoning for one earlier.
a) will   (b) might   c) can

JENNY: There's a taxi outside. Whose is it?
TOM: I'm not sure. I think it (1) . . . be
John's. He was telephoning for one earlier.
a) will   b) might   c) can

JENNY: Is there anyone else still here?
TOM: No. Only John.
JENNY: Well, then it (2) . . . be his.
a) must   b) won't   c) mustn't

John, I think your taxi has arrived.
JOHN: I'm coming. Thanks for the party. It was great.
TOM: That's O.K. Oh, wait a moment. Do you know whose jacket this is?
JOHN: I think Martin was wearing something like that.
It (3) . . . be his.
a) can't   b) will   c) could

(John leaves)
JENNY: Goodness. I'm tired. What's the time?
TOM: It's two fifteen.
JENNY: It (4) . . . be that late! When I looked at my watch a few moments ago, it was only one o'clock!
a) can't   b) won't   c) mustn't

TOM: Well, I'm sorry but that's the time.
JENNY: I forgot to tell you. The builders (5) . . . here at eight tomorrow morning.
a) come   b) are   c) will be

TOM: That's too bad because I (6) . . . be asleep!
a) can   b) 'll   c) must

2 Some people are wondering why their friend has not yet arrived at a meeting place. Rewrite the sentences using *may* or *might*.

Example
1 'Perhaps he doesn't know the way.'
1 *He may not know the way.*

1 'Perhaps he doesn't know the way.'
2 'Perhaps he's ill.'
3 'Perhaps his watch is slow.'
4 'Perhaps his train is late.'
5 'Perhaps there's a traffic jam.'

3 Report what the people are saying.

Example
1 'Go away!' (She/him)
1 *She told him to go away.*

1 'Go away!' (She/him)
2 'Could you speak more slowly, please?' (He/her)
3 'Don't be late back!' (He/her)
4 'Can you take us to Piccadilly Circus, please?' (They/him)
5 'Please don't leave the plane yet.' (She/them)

4 Rearrange the sentences to make a telephone conversation.

Example
1 *(E) Hello, can I speak to Diana, please?*

A: Yes, of course. What shall I tell her?
B: Thanks very much. Goodbye.
C: No, I'm afraid she's out. Who's speaking?
D: O.K. I'll tell her.
E: Hello, can I speak to Diana, please?
F: It's Cathy here.
G: Goodbye.
H: Can you ask her to phone me before nine o'clock this evening?
I: Oh, O.K. Can you give her a message from me?
J: Oh, hello, Cathy. No, I'm afraid Diana won't be back until seven o'clock.

5 Write sentences using one of these verbs in each sentence.

look sound taste smell feel seem

Example
1 This fish/delicious
1 This fish tastes delicious.

1 This fish/delicious
2 Her perfume/disgusting
3 That dress/expensive
4 This record/awful
5 This silk blouse/soft
6 Her boyfriend/very pleasant

6 Choose the odd word out.

Example
1 delicious (disgusting) mouth-watering appetizing.

1 delicious disgusting mouth-watering appetizing
2 fireplace ornament priest vase
3 taste comfort sound smell
4 tea can jar box
5 monsoon hurricane storm grain
6 pilot prayer cockpit aeroplane
7 frustrated disappointed wonderful anxious

7 Complete the sentences using *a*, *an*, *the* or no article.

Example
1 Stephen is . . . actor in . . . Royal Shakespeare Company.
1 Stephen is an actor in the Royal Shakespeare Company.

1 Stephen is . . . actor in . . . Royal Shakespeare Company.
2 She plays . . . violin beautifully.
3 Last night we had . . . dinner in . . . Italian restaurant.
4 In Finland and the Soviet Union people eat . . . reindeer as . . . special dish.
5 As a general rule, I don't like . . . background music.
6 . . . monsoons occur frequently in . . . tropical countries.
7 . . . hurricanes which hit the Caribbean in 1988 were . . . worst on record.
8 Do you ever get . . . nightmares?

CHECK YOUR PROGRESS

Add up your score. How well did you do?

Problem exercises . . .

LEARNING TO LEARN 5: Reading

Reading in a foreign language is one of the best ways to improve your ability. Here are some tips to help you read more easily and effectively:

1 Think before you start reading. Does the title tell you what the text is going to be about?
2 When you see a new word, don't look it up in a dictionary immediately. First try to guess its meaning from the context. Often you will find that it isn't necessary to know the meaning of some words.
3 Try to see and read whole phrases or sentences rather than individual words. This will help you to understand the text better.
4 Write down in your notebook any words which you think are useful or interesting to learn.
5 Try to read simple books or magazines in your spare time. And remember that you don't have to finish a book if you don't like it!

Preview

UNITS 26-30

Lisa is writing a letter to a friend in Australia. Match the parts of her letter with the correct photographs.

A I was surprised to hear about your sister. She isn't really going to cycle across China on a tandem, is she? She must be mad!

B There's a lot of interest in Australia here, although people don't think we have any history. What about the Aborigines, I say!

C Everyone is much more formal here. They usually shake hands when they meet people for the first time.

D I'm really pleased I'm going there. It's a country I've always wanted to visit.

E You like motor racing, don't you? Well, this will make you envious. I went to a Grand Prix at Brands Hatch on Saturday. I saw Ayrton Senna and Alain Prost. Terrific!

In Units 26–30 you will learn how to:

– check facts with question tags
– show surprise
– connect ideas with relative clauses
– make comparisons
– express contrast with *although* and *however*

Ayrton Senna is Brazilian, isn't he?

Yes, I think so.

AYRTON SENNA

Some say he is a genius, others call him arrogant. What is certainly true is that Ayrton Da Silva Senna is the fastest man in motor racing. He won the World Championship in 1988 and 1990 and he has won more than twenty Grand Prix altogether.

Ayrton Senna was born on 21st March 1960, in Brazil. At 5ft 9in (1m 76cm) Ayrton is a little taller than most other racing drivers. He is good-looking, with short, wavy, dark hair and dark brown eyes.

Senna does not like to talk about his private life. His marriage in the early 1980s lasted a year. 'To be married to a Formula One driver,' he says, 'is an impossible lifestyle for a wife. But I will get married again.'

He has an older sister and a younger brother. His parents live in a large house in the north of São Paulo but Senna himself lives in Monaco, in Europe.

As far as hobbies go, he likes flying model planes. He also enjoys jet-skiing on water and flying with his father over the cattle country which his family owns in Brazil.

What motivates him to win? 'Driving doesn't seem like a job. I started driving when I was four. I love feeling the power of the engine and the wind in my face. When I drive, I experience new sensations and I always want more. That is my motivation.'

The Brazilian is not very popular with his fellow drivers. Alain Prost, the French driver, says: 'Ayrton has a small problem. He thinks he can't kill himself because he believes in God. In the world of Formula One racing, that is very dangerous.' ∎

Before you read

Is motor racing popular in your country?
Do you like it? Why?/Why not?
Who is the top racing driver in your country?

1 READING

Read about Ayrton Senna and complete his fact file.

Date and place of birth:	. . .
Brothers and sisters:	. . .
Status: single? ☐	
married? ☐	
divorced? ☐	
Height:	. . .
Appearance:	. . .
Hobbies:	. . .
Parents' home:	. . .
Senna's present home:	. . .
Age when first started driving:	. . .
Major victories:	. . .

GRAMMAR FOCUS: Question tags

Question tags are used to check facts. With a positive sentence, you use a negative tag. With a negative sentence, you use a positive tag. The tag uses the auxiliary verb, e.g. *is, are, was, were, have, can, do, does, did.*

Your name **is** Ayrton, **isn't** it?
You **weren't** there, **were** you?
You **live** in Brazil, **don't** you?
You **didn't** arrive on Saturday, **did** you?
You**'ve been** to Rio, **haven't** you?

What's the difference in meaning?
1 Do you live in Brazil?
2 You live in Brazil, don't you?

2 Complete the sentences with the correct question tag.

1 You're over twenty, . . . you?
2 He isn't married, . . . he?
3 She's got two children, . . . she?
4 You like motor racing, . . . you?
5 He was their best driver, . . . he?
6 He didn't crash, . . . he?

3 In pairs, ask and answer about Ayrton Senna using question tags.

A: He comes from Brazil, doesn't he?
B: Yes, he was born in São Paulo.
A: He's over thirty, isn't he?
B: Yes, he's (. . .).

He comes from Brazil.
He is over thirty.
He isn't an only child.
He was married once.
He's quite tall.
He's got dark hair.
He likes model planes.
His parents live in Brazil.
He doesn't live with them.
He drives very fast.
He started driving when he was very young.
He has won the World Championship.

4 Note down five or six facts that you think are correct about someone in the class. Then, in pairs, check the facts, using question tags.

A: You were born in 1969, weren't you?
B: That's right./No, I was born in 1968.

5 VOCABULARY

Rearrange the letters to find the sports.

OLFG NGXOBI SITNEN LLAYEVBOLL
LLAOFBTO NGIIKS

1 Golf

6 About you

Which sports do you like watching?
Which sport do you like doing?
Do you like doing it because you want
   to keep fit or because you enjoy it?

7 In pairs, discuss which sports you think are:

boring to watch   dangerous   expensive
exciting to watch   excellent for keeping fit

A: I think football is boring to watch.
B: So do I./I don't think it's boring at all! I
   think it's exciting.

8 WRITING

Write a short description of a famous sports
personality in your country.

PARAGRAPH 1
Say who she/he is and why she/he is famous.

PARAGRAPH 2
Give some details of the person's
background, family and hobbies.

PARAGRAPH 3
Say where the person lives now, and what
her/his ambition is.

-27-
Surprise

Before you listen

Look at the newspaper headline below.
What do you think the article is about?

1 ▣ DIALOGUE

**Listen and find out what actually
happened to the captain in the headline.**

JANE: Good heavens! Look at this! It says a
pilot was nearly sucked out of the
window of his plane while it was in
mid-air!

BOB: No! Really! He wasn't, was he?

JANE: Yes, it says he was hanging out of the
window while the plane was 23,000
feet in the air!

BOB: I don't understand. The window didn't
break, did it?

JANE: Yes it did, apparently.

BOB: You're joking! Let's have a look.

2 READING

**Rearrange the paragraphs below in the
correct order.**

3 VOCABULARY

**Complete the sentences with the correct
form of the following words from the text.**

miraculous   suck   grab   narrow   shatter

1 He suddenly . . . the child as it walked into
the road.
2 When I turned and knocked the table, the
vase fell and . . . on the floor.
3 We were getting very short of water when
. . . it began to rain.
4 Children love to . . . drinks through a
straw.
5 The Russian swimmer, Yuri Konstantin,
only . . . won the 200 metres freestyle.

Captain sucked out of window at 23,000 feet

By John [A] Miraculously, Tim escaped with only minor injuries.

[B] While on a flight from Birmingham
to Malaga, the cockpit window on
Flight BA5390 shattered at 23,000ft.
The captain was sucked out of his
seat into the hole.

which old even been utine riday. was from

[C] The stewards held on to the
captain's legs until the co-pilot
landed the plane safely at
Southampton airport fifteen
minutes later.

hat moment,

[D] He immediately dropped the tray
and grabbed the captain's legs while
another steward strapped himself
into the pilot's seat.

By chance, one of the stewards was
serving tea in the cockpit when it
happened. [E]

legs him, the

[F] Tim Lancaster, an airline pilot,
narrowly escaped being sucked to
his death yesterday.

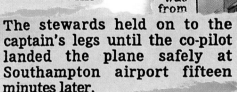

85

COMMUNICATION FOCUS
Showing surprise

With an expression
Good heavens!   You're joking! (informal)
What a surprise!   No, really!

With a question tag
The window didn't break, did it?
He wasn't, was he?

4 ▣ SPEECHWORK

Listen and repeat these question tags. Try to sound surprised each time.

It didn't break, did it? You aren't ill, are you?
You weren't, were you?
You haven't, have you?

5 ROLEPLAY

Student A meets Student B in the street. They haven't seen each other for ages.

A: Good heavens! It's Jenny Robb, isn't it?
B: Angela! What a surprise! It must be two years since we last met!

STUDENT A	STUDENT B
Express surprise. Identify and greet B.	
	Greet A. Express surprise. Say how long it is since you last met.
Agree. Ask how B is.	
	Reply. Ask what A is doing now.
Say that you are going to work in the USA next year.	
	Express surprise and ask why.
Explain what sort of work you are going to do there.	
	Express interest, then apologise and say that you must go. Say what the time is.
Express surprise and say goodbye.	

6 In pairs, respond with surprise to each headline.

A: It says here that Russia is going to join the European Community.
B: Good heavens! It isn't, is it?

1 McCARTNEY AND PAVAROTTI IN CONCERT
IT WAS revealed yesterday that Paul McCartney has invited Luciano Pavarotti to do a concert with him.
The concert, in aid of the Brazilian rain forests,

2 BRITAIN SLOWLY SINKING
By Leo Morris
A TOP secret government report today says that Britain is slowly sinking into the sea.

3 Chinese to be world language
THE members of the United Nations predicted that Chinese will be the world language by the middle of the next century.

4 Pope to visit Australia
THE POPE is going to visit Australia for the first time next May, according to sources in the Vatican.

5 Woman throws away Van Gogh painting by mistake
A TEXAS woman threw away a priceless Van Gogh painting last week because 'it didn't match the colour scheme' in her sitting room. The painting, worth an estimated $20 million,

6 Lost Beethoven symphony found in attic
ACCORDING to reliable sources in Munich, a German grandmother has found a 'lost' Beethoven symphony in her attic. Music historians

7 Olympic games cancelled
In a surprise announcement, the Olympic Committee have cancelled the next Olympics because of political unrest.

8 Russia to join EC
RUSSIA is going to join the European Community, according to Tass.

7 In groups, think of three imaginary headlines with surprising news. Choose the funniest to write on the board.

-28-
Everything you want

1 📼 DIALOGUE

Josh is at the office party at Work International.

LISA: Hi! I'm Lisa, Clare's niece. I'm from Australia.
JOSH: Yes, I can hear.
LISA: Come on! My accent's not that strong.
JOSH: How long have you lived in Australia?
LISA: All my life. I was born there.
JOSH: So you're here for a visit.
LISA: That's right. Have you ever been to Australia?
JOSH: No, but it's a part of the world I'd like to visit one day.
LISA: Well, it's got everything you want – sun, beaches, culture, wildlife . . . It's a great country. What about you? Are you British?
JOSH: Yes, I was born and brought up in England but my parents are from India, from the Punjab. They came over to England in the 1960s.
LISA: A German girl I know went to India for a holiday last year. She says it's the most exciting holiday she's ever had.
JOSH: Actually, I've only ever been there once!

Listen and answer *True* or *False*. Then correct the statements which are false.

1 Lisa has an English accent.
2 Lisa was born in Australia.
3 Josh has never been to Australia.
4 Josh was born in India.
5 Josh has Indian parents.
6 A friend of Lisa's had a wonderful holiday in Germany.
7 Josh has been to India several times.

GRAMMAR FOCUS
Defining relative clauses omitting *who*, *that* and *which*

The relative pronouns *who, that* and *which* can be omitted if they are objects of the verb in a defining relative clause.

A German girl (whom/ that) I know went to India for a holiday last year.
It's got everything (that) you want.
It's the most exciting holiday (that) she's ever had.

Note
Whom is the object form of *who*. It is used in written English but rarely in spoken English.

2 Which of these relative pronouns can you omit?

1 The woman *that* Bob married is English.
2 The man *who* lives next door is an artist.
3 The hotel *which* we stayed in was very comfortable.
4 It's the most spectacular view *that* you've ever seen.
5 She works for a company *which* sells computers.

3 Link the sentences with a relative clause.

1 I enjoyed the film I saw yesterday.

1 I enjoyed the film. I saw it yesterday.
2 We liked the Dutch people. We met them on holiday.
3 I have just finished the book. You gave it to me for my birthday.
4 Who has taken the magazines? I left them on the table.
5 Have you collected the bag? You left it in the theatre.

4 VOCABULARY

Sort the adjectives in the box into three columns: *Positive*, *Negative* or *Neutral*.

POSITIVE	NEGATIVE	NEUTRAL
beautiful	boring	unusual

beautiful unusual impressive boring
elegant different comfortable
exciting uncomfortable difficult useful
useless interesting tiring spectacular

Which of the adjectives can be paired as opposites?
boring – interesting

5 🔲 SPEECHWORK

Where does the main stress go on the adjectives in Exercise 4? Listen and check. Repeat the words as you hear them. Now group the words into four different stress patterns based on the following:

1 BORing   2 BEAUtiful
3 unUsual   4 unCOMfortable

6 WRITING

Use the model paragraph below to write paragraphs about other places. Change the words after each number with suitable words from the appropriate column.

[1]*Sydney* is one of the most exciting cities I've ever been to. The hotel [2]*I stayed in* was very [3]*comfortable*. Some [4]*Australian* people I met took me to see [5]*the opera house,* which is a very [6]*unusual building*. They also took me to see [7]*the outback*. [8]*The wildlife* is spectacular. [9]*Australia* is definitely a place I'd like to visit again.

*outback = the Australian countryside

1	2	3
Rome	you mentioned	elegant
Paris	I found	cheap
Delhi	I spent the week in	cool

4	5	6
Italian	The Colosseum	old building
French	Notre Dame	beautiful church
Indian	the Taj Mahal	impressive monument

7	8	9
the country	the scenery is	Italy
the Loire Valley	the chateaux are	France
the Himalayas	the mountains are	India

Rome is one of the most . . .

Now imagine that someone is visiting your country or city for the first time. Write a similar paragraph about it.

Diana Weston from Brooklyn, New York

BRITAIN

FIRST IMPRESSIONS

'**M**y first impression of Britain is that people are much more formal. For example, in the States we use first names almost immediately but here I have to be more careful. And British people are generally more polite. A New Yorker says: "Give me the check, will you!" when he finishes a meal but here in Britain they say: "Excuse me. Do you think you could give me the bill?"

I don't find a lot of difference in prices. They're about the same as in the States, I guess. It's the same with accommodation. I think it's a bit cheaper in London than in New York but there's not a lot of difference. One thing is certain, though, London is not as violent as New York. Some friends of mine who live in the Bronx have four locks on their door! I also prefer the subway here. It's cleaner and quieter, although the service isn't as efficient. On the whole, though, London is more polluted than New York because every-one there has to use lead-free petrol but in Britain it's not compulsory.

When it comes to work and business, my impression is that the British are much less hardworking than Americans. Sometimes I think the British don't know what a day's work means. '

—29—
Comparison

Before you read

Have you met any American or Japanese people?
What do you think their lifestyles are like?

1 READING

Read what two visitors think of life in Britain then complete the chart to compare the two impressions. In what areas do the two people have the same/different views?

BRITAIN	AN AMERICAN VIEW	A JAPANESE VIEW
The people:	more formal	. . .
	. . .	——
Clothes:	——	. . .
Prices:	. . .	. . .
Accommodation:	. . .	. . .
Violence:	. . .	. . .
Pollution:	. . .	. . .
Business attitudes:	. . .	. . .

GRAMMAR FOCUS: Comparison

Comparative forms

Comparative adjectives are formed by adding *-er* to the end of shorter adjectives and by putting *more* or *less* in front of longer adjectives.

high – high**er**
polluted – **more** polluted
expensive – **less** expensive

Modifiers: *much* and *a bit*

Prices in Japan are **much** higher than in London.
Food is **a bit** cheaper in the USA.
The Japanese are **much** more hardworking than the British.
People are **much** less formal in the USA than in Britain.

As . . . as/the same as

London isn't **as** violent **as** New York.
The price of food is about **the same (as** in New York).

Mr Yama from Osaka

'The prices here are about the same as in Japan, except for accommodation. In Japan the cost of accommodation is very high, much higher than in Britain. You also get more for your money here. For example, the houses, the flats and the gardens are much bigger. There is more open space here, too. In London there are lots of parks and the city isn't as polluted as Tokyo. However, I think society here is more violent. You read every day in the newspapers about some violence on the streets.

As for the people, I think the British are less formal, not only in the way they behave, but also in the way they dress. People wear much more casual clothes here than in Japan.

When it comes to business, the Japanese work longer hours than the British, often twelve hours a day. But the amusing thing for us is that the British change jobs much more frequently than we do. In Japan you usually stay in the same company for your whole working life. '

2 LISTENING

Now listen to Diana comparing restaurants in New York and London and note what she says about the food, the portions and the prices.

3 What are the comparative forms of these adjectives?

high fast formal expensive slow polluted casual
quiet polite big violent cheap easy

4 SPEECHWORK

Which syllables are stressed in these phrases?

much higher   much warmer   a bit easier   a bit older
much nicer   not as attractive   not as expensive

Now listen and see if you were right.

5 In pairs, use the notes and the ratings to give Lisa's opinion of Australia in comparison with Britain.

YOU: What are the people like in Australia?
LISA: I think they're much friendlier (than in Britain).

Australia

The people/++ friendly
The pace of life/+ slow
The choice of food/− wide
The standard of living/+ high
The climate/++ good
The cultural life/− − varied
Television programmes/− −
   interesting

Ratings	
+	-er/more
+ +	much -er/ much more
−	not as . . . as/less
− −	much less

6 About you

Use the ideas in Exercises 1 and 5 to compare your country with life in Britain.

7 WRITING

Before you write

Note how *for example, as for* and *when it comes to . . .* are used.

Food is more expensive here. **For example**, *a litre of milk costs £1.* **As for** *clothes, they are much more expensive here.* **When it comes to** *transport . . .*

You have invited a foreign guest to stay with you. Write a letter describing some of the differences your guest might notice in your country.

PARAGRAPH 1
Accommodation and cost of living
PARAGRAPH 2
Food and/or meal times
PARAGRAPH 3
Transport and traffic

Any-
icans
Sup-
office
New
which
o the
s and
rally
ound
must
more
d at
n the
nib-
in a
stop
diffe-
rging
only
be to
n the

eans,
rking
con-
t for
how,
rney,
de to
had a
posite

-30-
Aborigines

❝ When Western people look at land, they ask the price. They think: "What can I build on it and how fast?" We see things differently. For us as Aborigines, land is mother, father, life itself. Land belongs to us. And we belong to the land. When we lose our land, we lose ourselves. ❞

Robert Kelly

THE AUSTRALIAN ABORIGINES

'Aborigines' are the first or original inhabitants of a country. The Australian Aborigines have lived in Australia for over 40,000 years. At one stage in their history there were possibly over a million Aborigines. However, when the first white settlers arrived in the 18th century and stole their land, many Aborigines died fighting to protect it. Today only about 100,000 survive. Although some still live a traditional life in remote desert areas of the Australian outback, many now live in poor conditions in cities and towns.

They have suffered for two hundred years from white exploitation. However, the Australian government has recently given some land back to them. This includes 'Uluru' (Ayers Rock), a huge rock in the centre of Australia, which is of sacred importance to the Aborigines.

Although winning back this land is encouraging, the Aboriginal people know there is a long way to go before they win back the rest of their land.

AUSTRALIA

● Ayers Rock   BRISBANE ●

● PERTH   SYDNEY ●
          ADELAIDE ●   CANBERRA ●
                    MELBOURNE ●

1 READING

Read and guess the meaning.

inhabitant settler protect survive
suffer exploitation sacred encouraging

Answer *True* or *False*.

1 Aborigines have only recently arrived in Australia.
2 The first settlers in Australia bought land from the Aborigines.
3 There were originally many more Aborigines than there are today.
4 Nearly all Aborigines today live in the outback.
5 The Aboriginal name for Ayers Rock is 'Uluru'.
6 Ayers Rock now belongs to the Aborigines.

GRAMMAR FOCUS
Although and *however*

Two contrasting sentences and ideas can be linked with *although* or *however*.

Although some still live a traditional life in the Australian outback, many now live in cities and towns.
=
Some still live a traditional life in the Australian outback. **However**, many now live in cities and towns.

Find other examples in the text of ideas linked with *although* **or** *however*.

2 ▣ LISTENING

Complete each line of this Aboriginal poem with one of the following words. Then listen and see if you were right.

me   gum tree   hue   kangaroo   singing
new   sea

'I am a child of the dreamtime people,
Part of the land like the old . . . ,
I am the river softly . . . ,
Chanting our songs on the way to the . . .
I awakened here when the earth was . . .
There was emu, wombat, . . .
No other man of a different . . .
I am the land and this land is . . .
I am Australia.'

An unknown poet

Glossary
dreamtime An Aboriginal word. It has nothing to do with sleep. It is used by Aborigines to describe the time when their ancestors walked about the earth.
gum tree An Australian eucalyptus tree.
hue A literary word meaning colour.

3 Use the notes to make sentences about Australia starting with *although*.

1 Australia/smallest continent/largest island in the world.
2 Total population/sixteen million/there are only 100,000 Aborigines.
3 Non-aboriginal history/only two hundred years old/Aboriginal history goes back over 40,000 years.
4 No lions and tigers/Australia/other unique wild animals like kangaroos, emus and wombats.

4 Make sentences from the notes, using *however*.

1 Aborigines have certainly lived in Australia for 40,000 years/they may have been there for much longer.
2 *Dreamtime* contains the word *dream*/it has nothing to do with sleep.
3 The first white settlers killed many Aborigines/more died from the diseases which the settlers brought with them.
4 Australian Aborigines have gained some land/they still have a long fight ahead.

5 What do you think?

Why do you think the Aboriginal people lost their land?
Where else have white people taken land from the original inhabitants?
What has happened to these people?

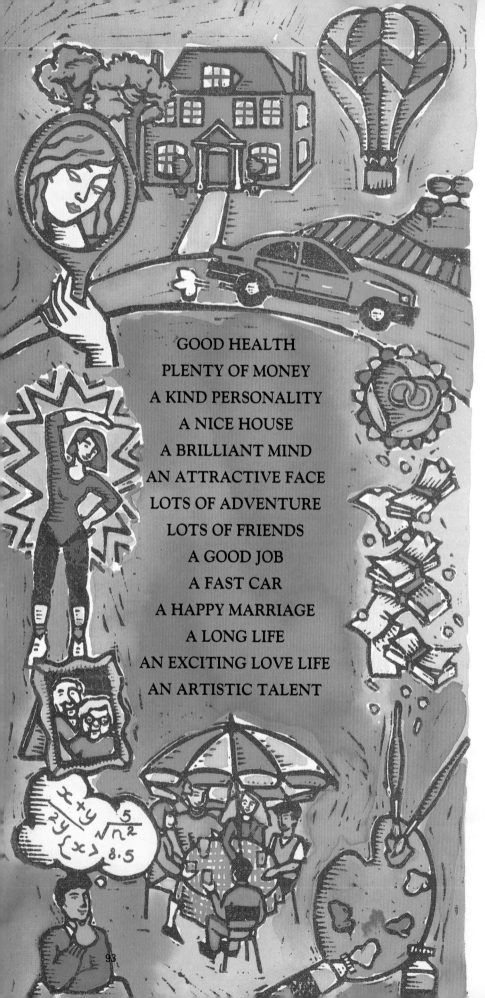

Fluency

UNITS 26–30

1 Imagine that you are allowed to have some of the gifts on the left for your birthday. Choose three gifts which you think are the most important or useful and three which are the least important or useful.

2 Compare your choice with other people in your group and agree on the three most important gifts. These phrases may help:

I think the most important thing in life is . . .
I think it's much more useful/ important to have . . . than . . .
. . . isn't as important as . . .
The one thing I'd like to have is . . .
The one I think is most/least important is . . .

3 ROLEPLAY

Roleplay the following conversations.

A telephone conversation with a friend

STUDENT A
It is your birthday. You want to invite some friends for a meal in a restaurant on Saturday night. Choose a restaurant and telephone your friend Student B.

STUDENT B
You are free on Saturday and would like to go to A's birthday meal. Find out when and where to meet.

GOOD HEALTH
PLENTY OF MONEY
A KIND PERSONALITY
A NICE HOUSE
A BRILLIANT MIND
AN ATTRACTIVE FACE
LOTS OF ADVENTURE
LOTS OF FRIENDS
A GOOD JOB
A FAST CAR
A HAPPY MARRIAGE
A LONG LIFE
AN EXCITING LOVE LIFE
AN ARTISTIC TALENT

A telephone conversation with a restaurant manager

STUDENT A

You want to book a table for four people for Saturday night. You phone the restaurant you have chosen.

STUDENT B

You are the restaurant manager. When people phone, you must find out what time they want to book a table for, how many people there will be in the group and the name of the person who is booking the table.

The birthday celebration in the restaurant

Choose one of the roles on the right, read your rolecard and then start the conversation, using the menu.

THE MILL

Menu

Starters

*Pate · Scottish smoked salmon
Spring vegetable soup*

Main course

*Steak au poivre · Fish of the day
Omelette with ham or wild mushrooms
Chicken Kiev · Vegetable lasagne*

Vegetables of the day

*All dishes served
with either rice or french fries*

Dessert

*Chocolate, Strawberry or Vanilla ice cream
Apple pie and cream · Fruit salad*

White or red wine · Champagne · Mineral water

HOST

- It is your birthday and you want to spend some money! You would like to start with champagne.
- You want everyone to choose different things from the menu.
- You do not want to talk about work.
- You frequently check that your guests are enjoying the meal.
- Towards the end of the meal, you announce your surprise engagement to a famous person. Your fiancé/fiancée is not with you tonight.

GUEST 1

- You are a vegetarian and you only like simple food.
- You work with the host and would like to discuss a work problem with him/her.
- You are fairly sure that the host's fiancé/ fiancée was in the newspapers yesterday and you check this with your host.
- You would like to get home as early as possible.

GUEST 2

- You love eating out in restaurants and enjoy advising people what to eat and drink.
- You are planning to go to Australia for a holiday. You are sure that Guest 3 has been to Australia and you want to know how much the airfare costs approximately and where he/she suggests you should go.
- You are very surprised about your host's choice of fiancé/fiancée.

GUEST 3

- You are not very hungry as you are recovering from a cold. You do not want to drink any alcohol.
- You spent two months in Sydney in Australia last year. You enjoyed it very much but you cannot remember the cost of the airfare.
- You like to ask people about television programmes they have seen.
- When you hear your host's news, you want to know where the fiancé/fiancée is.

Check

1 Complete the sentences using a question tag.

Example
1 It's a beautiful day, . . .
1 *It's a beautiful day, isn't it?*

1 It's a beautiful day, . . .
2 You weren't here yesterday, . . .
3 She went to university in 1978, . . .
4 They aren't leaving now, . . .
5 You haven't been here before, . . .
6 She's got a job now, . . .
7 You live quite near me, . . .
8 He doesn't smoke, . . .
9 I've made a mistake, . . .
10 You can come on Wednesday, . . .

2 Write sentences reacting to the statements with surprise.

Example
1 I've won £100!
1 *You haven't, have you!*

1 I've won £100!
2 She's had another baby.
3 He was at school with my father.
4 I fell asleep during that film.
5 She feels sick.
6 I'm hungry again.
7 I can speak Chinese.

3 Complete the sentences with a relative clause. Use the statements in the box.

We met them on holiday.
You are watching it.
I borrowed it from the library.
Your husband was talking to her.
I bought it for your birthday.

Example
1 The book . . . is very exciting.
1 *The book I borrowed from the library is very exciting.*

1 The book . . . is very exciting.
2 That nice couple . . . can't come.
3 What happened to the watch . . . ?
4 What's the film . . . ?
5 Who's the girl . . . ?

4 Complete the sentences with *who, which* or *that*. Write *that* in brackets (*that*) if it is not necessary.

Example
1 This is the most delicious ice cream . . . I've ever tasted.
1 *This is the most delicious ice cream (that) I've ever tasted.*

1 This is the most delicious ice cream . . . I've ever tasted.
2 There's a shop next door . . . sells jeans.
3 Everyone . . . has been to Australia loves it.
4 I want you to tell me everything . . . you know.
5 Have you met the man . . . lives next door?
6 I'm afraid that's all . . . I know.

5 Complete the sentences using *much* or *a bit* and a comparative form of the adjective.

1 This test is (a bit/easy) than the last one.
1 *This test is a bit easier than the last one.*

1 This test is (a bit/easy) than the last one.
2 The weather is (much/warm) today.
3 I think this video sounds (much/interesting) than that one.
4 This jacket is quite tight. Have you got anything (a bit/large)?
5 The Andes are (much/high) than any mountains in our country.
6 Why not use this bed? It's (a bit/comfortable) than that old one.

6 Complete the sentences with *as, so* or *than*.

Example
1 Birmingham isn't as large . . . London.
1 *Birmingham isn't as large as London.*

1 Birmingham isn't as large . . . London.
2 You shouldn't eat . . . many cakes!
3 You're not . . . tall . . . I thought.
4 Your bag looks exactly the same . . . mine.
5 The hotel is much more expensive this year . . . last year.

7 Complete the crossword.

¹S	U	²R	P	R	I	³S	E	⁴D	
U						⁵			⁶
R		⁷		⁸					
⁹V							¹⁰		
I			¹¹						
¹²V		¹³					¹⁴		
E				¹⁵					
¹⁶D	¹⁷		¹⁸	¹⁹		²⁰			
	²¹		²²		²³				
²⁴		²⁵							

CLUES

Across
1 You sound . . . to see me! (9)
5 Opposite of *bottom*. (3)
7 To break into many pieces. (7)
9 Athletes often wear this. (4)
10 Rhymes with *go*. (2)
11 You turn this on to get water. (3)
12 A win. (7)
14 Object pronoun from *I*. (2)
16 How . . . you do? (2)
18 The person who flies an aeroplane. (5)
21 A wild animal. (4)
23 Goodbye. Take . . . ! (4)
24 Short for *compact disc*. (2)
25 Opposite of *men*. (5)

Down
1 Managed to stay alive. (8)
2 Could you . . . this letter for me, please? (4)
3 Short for English Teaching Theatre. (4)
4 What . . . your father do? (4)
6 Kept away from danger. (9)
8 Used to carry food and drink from one place to another. (4)
11 A short journey. (4)
13 You must be able to . . . the ball a long way if you play cricket. (5)
15 When you write an essay you should make a . . . first. (4)
17 Not young. (3)
19 Something which can melt. (3)
20 I'll come on either Monday . . . Tuesday. (2)
22 A negative answer. (2)

8 Complete the sentences using *although* and a sentence from the box.

Example
1 . . . I got there in ten minutes.
1 *Although the traffic was bad, I got there in ten minutes.*

She has never been to Spain.
He earns quite a lot.
The traffic was bad.
I was very tired.
The water was quite cold.
She had the qualifications.

1 . . . I got there in ten minutes.
2 She didn't get the job . . .
3 I couldn't go to sleep . . .
4 . . . she can speak fluent Spanish.
5 We swam several times . . .
6 . . . he never seems to have any money.

CHECK YOUR PROGRESS

Add up your score. How well did you do?

Problem exercises . . .

LEARNING TO LEARN 6: Writing

Many people get a headache as soon as they think about writing, even in their own language! But writing is much easier if you *plan* what you are going to write. Here are some useful tips:

1 Think about what you want to say. You may like to discuss this with a partner.
2 Note down everything to do with the topic. Then cross out what is not relevant.
3 Make a list of words or expressions you would like to include, e.g. *in fact, on the whole*.
4 Make a plan. Decide what you want to say in each paragraph.
5 Write your first draft and check it for grammar, punctuation and spelling mistakes.
6 Read it aloud. Does it sound English? Can you join some of the sentences?
7 Write a second draft and note any questions to your teacher in the margin, e.g. *Is this the right word? Should I use the past continuous instead here?*

Preview

UNITS 31–35

⌨ Match the text with the photographs. Then listen and see if you were right.

A Clues are checked and examined in the laboratory after a crime.

B – What was the concert like?
– Great! But it was so crowded that we couldn't get near the stage.

C When I got to the station, the train had just left.

D If you wear a wetsuit, you won't get cold.

E – That office block used to be a theatre.
– When was that?
– Not so long ago.

In Units 31–35 you will learn how to:

– talk about past habits and situations
– talk about results
– talk about future events and their possible consequences
– describe background events
– describe processes

-31-
Past habits

1 🔲 DIALOGUE

JOSH: There's the school I used to go to when I was little.

EVA: It looks a bit old and depressing!

JOSH: I know but it's all right inside! And do you see that house over there?

EVA: The one with the white fence?

JOSH: Yes. I used to live there. My parents were quite poor then. We didn't use to have a washing machine or anything like that.

EVA: How did you manage?

JOSH: We used to go to the launderette every week. But it's different now. Dad works at the airport and Mum works in a shop.

EVA: So, they're doing all right.

JOSH: Yes, Mum's got a washing machine and a dishwasher as well!

Listen and answer *True* or *False*.

1 Josh lived near his school when he was younger.
2 The school was very modern.
3 Josh's parents always had quite a lot of money.
4 They washed all their clothes by hand.
5 Both Josh's parents have got jobs now.

GRAMMAR FOCUS: *Used to*

The modal verb *used to* is used to describe past habits and facts which are no longer true.

Positive
I used to live in that house (but I don't now).

Negative
We didn't use to have a washing machine (but we do now).

Question	*Short answer*
Did you use to cycle to school?	Yes, I did. No, I didn't.

What's the difference in meaning?
1 I usually cycle to work.
2 I used to cycle to work.

2 In pairs, ask each other about your past life. Use *So . . . /Nor . . .* for any situations or experiences you have in common.

Talk about:
– your appearance
– your school life
– your spare time activities

A: What did you use to look like as a child?
B: I used to have blonde hair.
A: So did I.
B: Did you use to wear glasses?

3 VOCABULARY

Match the words in the box below with the pictures of the modern inventions.

1 a vacuum cleaner

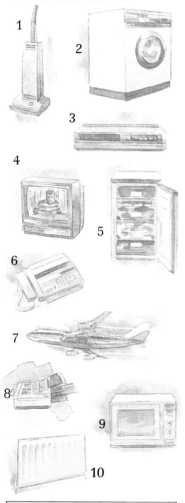

deep freeze   telephone
microwave   television
aeroplane   video   fax
vacuum cleaner
central heating
washing machine

4 Look at the items in Exercise 3. Say how people managed without them in the past. What did they use to do?

1 (a vacuum cleaner) They used to sweep carpets and floors by hand.

FROM THE PUNJAB TO DERBYSHIRE

STEVE CURRAN MEETS A NEW MEMBER OF THE POLICE FORCE

Surojit Sen seems like a typical British 'bobby' with his dark blue uniform and his Derbyshire accent. But seventeen years ago he arrived in Britain from India at the age of nine, not knowing a word of English.

'My father came here and started a restaurant in Derby. When the business was secure, he sent for the rest of our family.'

At home, Surojit, his two brothers and one sister used to speak Punjabi. 'My mother still doesn't speak very good English. As soon as we learnt English, we used to interpret for her. We all had to help in the restaurant. We used to cook, clean and do the accounts. I never used to get to bed before 2 a.m.'

When he was a teenager, Surojit's friends used to tease him because of his Indian accent so he made up his mind to lose it. 'I wanted to play football or go into a pub without people noticing me.' After leaving school, he decided to join the police. 'I wanted to do something worthwhile for the community.'

Surojit knows of only one or two more Indian police officers but he hopes there will be more soon. 'Honesty and hard work are a great part of Indian culture. I am proud to be a policeman and I enjoy my job very much. But I would like to see Indian people more integrated in the British community.'

5 READING

Read about a police officer and complete the information.

Name: Surojit Sen	First language:
Job:	Father's job:
Nationality:	Previous work experience:

6 Answer the questions about Surojit using *used to* where appropriate.

1 What language did Surojit speak at home?
2 How did he help in the restaurant?
3 Why do you think he was tired in the morning?
4 Why did he want to lose his Indian accent?
5 Why did he want to join the police?

7 About you

Did anyone use to tease you at your school? If so, why?
How did you use to help your parents when you were younger?

2

Some Irish people I met in Dublin invited me to spend a few days in their cottage near the Atlantic coast. I tell you, it was so wild and primitive that there wasn't even electricity or running water! And I had such an amazing experience there. I must tell you about it. We went for a long walk one day and suddenly we found a long, white empty beach. It was like a paradise beach. We started walking along it and then a few minutes later we heard a noise like hundreds of trumpeting elephants. It was so loud I thought I was going crazy! We climbed some rocks and I could hardly believe my eyes when I got to the top. To my surprise, there was another long white beach and on it were hundreds of seals! It was such an amazing sight that I took a whole roll of film. Fortunately, I had a spare one with me. I'll show you the photos when I get back.

1 ▭ READING

Read part of Lisa's letter to a friend. Put the following events in the correct order.

1 Lisa took a lot of photographs.
2 They went for a walk one day.
3 She went to stay with them in their cottage near the Atlantic coast.
4 They climbed some rocks.
5 Lisa made some Irish friends.
6 They saw a beautiful beach covered in seals.
7 They heard a strange noise.

GRAMMAR FOCUS
so . . . (that)/such . . . (that)

It's **such** a beautiful beach.
They're **such** beautiful animals.
It's **so** beautiful.

**Look at how *so* and *such* are used.
Which is used before an adjective?
Which is used before an adjective +
noun?**

So and *such* are often followed by a clause
of result or consequence beginning with
that. Sometimes, the word *that* is omitted.

It was **so** loud (**that**) I thought I was going
crazy.
It was **such** an amazing sight (**that**) I took
a whole roll of film.

2 ▣ SPEECHWORK

**Listen and note the stressed words in
these sentences.**

I was so tired that I fell asleep.
He was such a nice man that I invited him to
lunch.
The room was so crowded that I felt ill.
They were such friendly people that I asked
them to tea.

Now listen and repeat the sentences.

**3 When she was in Ireland, Lisa went to a
rock concert. Write sentences about it
using *so . . . that*.**

1 The concert was so popular that we had to
queue all night for tickets.

1 The concert/popular/ /we had to queue all
night for tickets.
2 We/late/ /we couldn't get seats near the
stage.
3 The video screens large/ /we could see the
band quite well.
4 The atmosphere/fantastic/ /the band
played for an extra hour.
5 The evening/hot/ /lots of people fainted.
6 The band/good/ /we would like to see
them again.

**Rewrite sentences 1, 4, 5 and 6 using
such (a) . . . that.**

1 It was such a popular concert that we had
to queue all night for tickets.

4 ▣ LISTENING

**Listen to Lisa's conversation with Clare
about the rock concert and note these
conversational expressions.**

Well, . . .   Oh? . . .   Er . . .   Anyway, . . .

**Listen again and write the sentences in
which the expressions occur.**

1 Well, Dublin, of course, . . .

**Which of the expressions indicate that the
speaker is:**

1 thinking about what to say?
2 starting to explain something?
3 interested and wants to hear more?
4 closing a topic of conversation and
starting a new one?

5 About you

What big pop concerts have there been
recently in your country?
Do you think that such large concerts are
enjoyable? Why?/Why not?
Have you been to any other event with a
large crowd? If so, what was it?

6 WRITING

Narrative expressions

```
a few seconds/minutes/hours/days later
to my surprise   suddenly   (un)fortunately
```

**Study how the words and phrases in the
box are used in Lisa's letter. Then
complete the paragraph below, choosing
a suitable word or phrase.**

'One day I was in the kitchen when . . . I
heard a noise in the sitting room. I went to
see what it was and, . . . , I saw a bird on the
floor. . . . , I was able to catch it. I opened the
window and . . . , it flew away.'

**Now write about a dramatic or surprising
incident. Use some of the structures in the
Focus box and some narrative
expressions.**

PARAGRAPH 1
Say where you were and what you were
doing at the time.
PARAGRAPH 2
Describe what happened.
PARAGRAPH 3
Describe your reaction and what you did as a
result.

-33-
What will happen if ...?

1 DIALOGUE

Clare is having a diving lesson.

INSTRUCTOR: Remember, come back up to the surface slowly and don't hold your breath.

CLARE: I see. What will happen if I come up too fast?

INSTRUCTOR: Your lungs will hurt. Don't try it. It can be very painful!

Listen and answer the questions.

1 What is Clare learning to do?
2 What does the instructor advise her to do?
3 What will happen if she doesn't do this?

GRAMMAR FOCUS
First conditional *if* clauses + future

The first conditional is used to describe a possible future event and its consequences.

Positive + Positive
If you come up too fast, your lungs will hurt.

Positive + Negative
If you come up slowly, your lungs won't hurt.

Negative + Negative
If you don't come up so fast, your lungs won't hurt.

What tense is the verb in the *if* clause?
What tense is the verb in the main clause?

Note
The first conditional tense is also often used to threaten or warn people, e.g. *If you don't go away, I'll call the police.*

2 SPEECHWORK

/əʊ/ as in *don't*

Which of these words have the same vowel sound as the word *don't*?

won't   want   phoned   home   lot   boat
gone   wrong   tone   won

Listen and see if you were right, then repeat these phrases.

If you don't phone, . . .
If you don't know, . . .
If you don't go home, . . .
If you don't phone, I won't know.

3 In pairs, make conversations with *if*.

1 A: Do you think you'll pass your driving test?
   B: I'm not sure. (pass/have a big party)
2 B: I think I've left my watch somewhere in your house.
   A: O.K. (find it/send it to you)
3 A: How are you getting on with the new computer?
   B: Fine. (need any help/call you)
4 B: How do you feel?
   A: Not too good. (not feel better soon/ telephone the doctor)
5 B: Can you get me the new Stephen King novel?
   A: Sure. (bookshop/have got/buy it for you)
6 A: They say the weather is going to change this afternoon.
   B: I hope not. (rain/be very annoyed)

4 VOCABULARY

Look at the photograph and find the diving equipment.

mask   flippers   wetsuit   weight belt

Look up these expressions in a dictionary.

to rinse out   to mist up   to sink

5 Use the chart below to give advice about scuba diving.

1 − wear a wetsuit   + get cold

If you don't wear a wetsuit, you'll get cold.

WETSUITS	
1 − wear a wetsuit	+ get cold
2 + wear a wetsuit	− cut yourself on rocks
MASKS AND FLIPPERS	
3 − rinse out your mask	+ mist up
4 + get hair in your mask	+ water come in
5 + use your flippers correctly	+ swim faster
BREATHING	
6 + breathe slowly	+ feel more comfortable
WEIGHTS	
7 − wear a weight belt	− move well underwater
8 + weights too heavy	+ sink to the bottom

6 🎧 LISTENING DIALOGUE

Before you listen

What new job has Josh got with Work International?
How do you think Eva feels when he goes away?

Listen and complete the dialogue.

JOSH: Are you ready for your driving test?
EVA: I'm not sure. If I . . . , . . . very lucky.
JOSH: I think . . . pass first time.
EVA: Maybe . . . talk about something else. What about the Latin American job? . . . decided to take it?
JOSH: The job in Venezuela? Yes, . . . wanted to go to Latin America.
EVA: But if you . . . , we . . . each other for over six months!
JOSH: I know, but it's a great chance. If I . . . it now, I . . . another chance. I'm sorry, Eva. Where . . . ?
EVA: Out! If you . . . me, . . . at Annika's.

7 WRITING

You are going on a class outing. (Where?) You have all arranged to meet at the main railway station. (When?) There is another train to the same place half an hour later. The organisers will wait for people who miss the first train. (Where?)

Write a note to another friend who wants to join the trip. Explain the arrangements and tell your friend what to do if anything goes wrong, for example, if he/she is late and misses the train.

Dear . . . ,
I'm glad you've decided to come with us on our trip to . . . These are the arrangements. We're meeting . . . If . . .

If Schmidt wants to win this race, he'll have to put his skates on.

Broken wedding plans

A FAIRY-TALE wedding in a pretty village just outside Paris was cancelled last Saturday when 27-year-old Hugh Baxter from Cambridge failed to turn up. Hugh said: 'The whole story is a nightmare. The wedding was on the Saturday morning and I had planned to drive to London on the Friday night and catch the overnight boat train to Paris. Unfortunately, I couldn't go earlier because my company had arranged an important business meeting for me on the Friday. Anyway, I left my house in plenty of time but there was a bad traffic jam on the motorway, which delayed me, so when I arrived at Victoria Station in London, the train for Paris had already left. I rushed to the airport to try to catch the 10.30 flight but they had just sold the last seat!'

Hugh's fiancée, 22-year-old Marie-Claire Duclos, commented: 'It is typical of an Englishman to put business before romance.' When asked if she was planning another date for the wedding, she said: 'I'm thinking about it.'

Past background

1 READING

Read and choose the right answer.

1 The wedding location was
   a) Cambridge.
   b) France.
   c) Victoria Station.

2 He arrived late at the station because
   a) he had an important meeting.
   b) he had an accident.
   c) there were long delays on the motorway.

3 He did not take the 10.30 flight from the airport because
   a) there were no places left on the flight.
   b) he didn't have enough money.
   c) he arrived too late and the plane had gone.

4 His fiancée
   a) has now decided not to get married.
   b) is trying to arrange another wedding as soon as possible.
   c) has not decided on another date for the wedding yet.

The past simple is used to talk about events which happened in the past.

He **arrived** at the station.

The past perfect simple is used to talk about events which happened before that time.

When he arrived at the station, the train **had left.**

This can be explained as follows:

Past time
9.05   The train left.
9.10   He arrived at the station.

What's the difference in meaning?
1 When he arrived, the train left.
2 When he arrived, the train had left.

2 How many examples of the past perfect tense can you find in the newspaper article?

3 Which event happened first?

1 I decided to buy John's car but he had already sold it.
2 She didn't recognise him after he had shaved off his beard.
3 He had spent the day in London so he was quite tired.

4 ⬛ LISTENING

Listen to another story about a wedding. Compare it with the story in Exercise 1. In what ways are they similar and in what ways are they different?

5 Imagine you have lost your watch. In pairs, use the cues to make conversations.

A: Did you catch the train?
B: No, by the time I got there, the train had already left.

1 Did you catch the train? (get there/leave)
2 Did you meet Mr Briggs? (arrive/go)
3 Did you see the football match? (turn on the TV/finish)
4 Did you get to the party in time? (turn up/everyone go home)
5 Did you get to the bank? (arrive/shut)

6 Complete the text, changing the verbs in brackets into the past simple or the past perfect.

'Last week I (have) a funny experience. I (be) on my own in the house. My husband (go away) on a business trip. The first evening I (be) rather tired as I (spend) the day shopping and cleaning. After supper I (watch) television and then (decide) to go to bed early. I (feel) quite safe because I (lock) all the doors and I (close) all the windows securely. I was just going to sleep when I (hear) the sound of men's voices, talking quietly. I (be) terrified. I (get) out of bed and (creep) downstairs. The voices were coming from the sitting room. I (open) the door, trembling, and then (laugh) with relief. In my tiredness I (forget) to turn off the television!'

Before you read

In which countries are earthquakes common?
Have you ever experienced one?
What happens to buildings during an earthquake?

7 READING

Read and answer the questions.

1 What had happened to Isadora's house during the first earthquake?
2 Where had her sister been?
3 Why couldn't she get through to Jon after the first earthquake?
4 Why couldn't she get through after the second earthquake?
5 What had Jon tried to do?

8 VOCABULARY

Complete the sentences with the correct form of the verbs in the box.

1 The boy was so frightened that he trembled with fear.

crack sway tremble
shake fall

1 The boy was so frightened that he . . . with fear.
2 During the earthquake the earth . . . quite violently.
3 Outside the trees were . . . in the wind.
4 Many buildings . . . to the ground.
5 The road ahead began to . . . into several pieces.

9 WRITING

Write a composition about 'A day I shall never forget'. Try to use some of these narrative expressions from the text in Exercise 7.

suddenly   fortunately
in the evening/morning
the next day   finally
then   to my great relief

I SHALL NEVER FORGET THAT DAY

ISADORA writes about the day when an earthquake struck her city

" I shall never forget that day. I woke up as usual at half past six in the morning, washed my face, had my breakfast and went to school. Everything was O.K. except for a strange feeling. Suddenly, the earth started to shake under my feet.

I wasn't frightened at that moment but when I saw the buildings were swaying I began to tremble with fear. Nature was angry with us. I had never seen rain like this before. I ran for home. Fortunately, everything was O.K. One of the bedroom walls had cracked but that was all. My sister, Anna, had been at the university when the earthquake happened but she didn't seem too frightened. I tried desperately to telephone my boyfriend, Jon, but I couldn't reach him. The lines were engaged.

In the evening, everything returned to normal. I went to sleep after midnight, thinking of Jon. The next day I found out there had been another earthquake, weaker than the first, at three o'clock in the morning. Fortunately I hadn't felt it and my grandparents hadn't woken me.

I finally got through to Jon's number but there was no answer; he wasn't at school either. I went to look for him. When I got to his house, I saw him. He was lying in the corner of the room by the telephone. He had tried to make a phone call but the wall above his head had fallen in. To my great relief he was still alive, although he was unconscious. It was the worst and the best moment of my life. "

THANK YOU RUSTY

By Don Baker

IT was a very special day yesterday for Rusty, a 9-year-old police sniffer dog. Most sniffer dogs retire at the age of 7, but Rusty has just retired after nearly 9 years' duty.

Rusty certainly ended his career with a bang. Last week Rusty and his trainer, Jim Turner, discovered 2 kilos of cocaine worth over £100,000 in an East London house. 'He's one of our best sniffer dogs,' says Jim. 'We're going to miss him.'

Rusty had a special party last night at a police dog training school near Bristol. Rusty's retirement present was a juicy bone and a new collar.

-35-
Dog detectives

Before you read

Do the police use dogs in your country? When and where do you use them?

Dog detectives behind the headlines

This week Steve Walters takes a look at the use of sniffer dogs in crime detection

SNIFFER DOGS are used by police and customs officers all over the world to detect drugs and explosives. Dogs have a far better sense of smell than people because the smell receptors at the top of a dog's nose are 100 times longer than in humans.

Training for a sniffer dog lasts 12 weeks. They are trained in two stages. First, the trainer teaches the dog to recognise a particular drug or explosive. He hides a sample of the drug or explosive inside a rolled-up newspaper or a rag, which is called a training aid. He places it where the dog can see it and tells the dog to bring the aid back. When it does so, he gives the dog a reward – usually a friendly fight with the trainer or a bone.

The dog soon learns to recognise the substance by its smell. The type of training aid is changed regularly but the smell always remains the same. In the second stage, the aid is hidden where the dog cannot see it. Smells such as perfumes, which some smugglers use to hide the smell of the drugs, are also used so that the dog becomes familiar with them.

Sniffer dogs are trained to detect 12 different types of explosives and four different types of drugs.

1 READING

Read the newspaper cutting about Rusty and correct these statements.

1 Rusty has just completed his training.
2 Most dogs retire at the age of nine.
3 Last week Rusty discovered some explosives.
4 Last night the dog trainers gave Rusty a birthday party.

Now read the other article and complete the information.

SNIFFER DOGS

Used by:
Main use:
Length of training:
Number of stages:
Types of training aids used:
Rewards given:
Number of substances dogs can detect:

2 VOCABULARY

Find words in the texts which have a similar meaning to the following:

1 to finish work permanently
2 to give a course of instruction
3 a part of a process
4 a piece of torn material or cloth
5 a return for doing something well
6 to discover something from clues

GRAMMAR FOCUS: Present passive

The passive is used when we are interested in the event or process itself, rather than the person who does it. The passive is formed by combining the appropriate tense of the verb *to be* with the past participle of the main verb. It is often followed by a phrase with *by*.

Active	Passive
The police **use** dogs to find drugs.	Dogs **are used** (by the police) to find drugs.

How many passive forms can you find in the text? What are they?

---

3 Rewrite the second paragraph of the main text using the passive.

They are trained in two stages. First, the dog is taught to . . .

4 In pairs, use the words in the box to talk about how people are punished in your country for different crimes.

A: What happens if you are caught driving over the speed limit?
B: You're fined./You're banned from driving for a year.

---
fine   ban from driving (for . . . years)
send to prison (for . . . years)

What happens in your country if you are caught:
– driving over the speed limit?
– drinking and driving?
– stealing?
– smuggling drugs?

5 🔲 LISTENING

Before you listen

What sort of clues do police look for at the scene of a crime?

Listen to a police officer talking about how fingerprints are used to solve a crime. Put the stages in the correct order.

A They cover the surfaces with fine powder to find fingerprints.
B The police search the scene of the crime in great detail.
C They compare them to fingerprints of suspects and known criminals.
D They place sticky tape over the fingerprints to lift them.
E They collect clues.
F They photograph the prints back in the laboratory.

6 WRITING

Rewrite the sentences from Exercise 5 in the correct order, using the present passive. Link the sentences with the time markers:

First . . . and . . .
Next . . .
Then . . .
After that . . .
Finally . . .

First the scene of the crime is searched in great detail and . . .

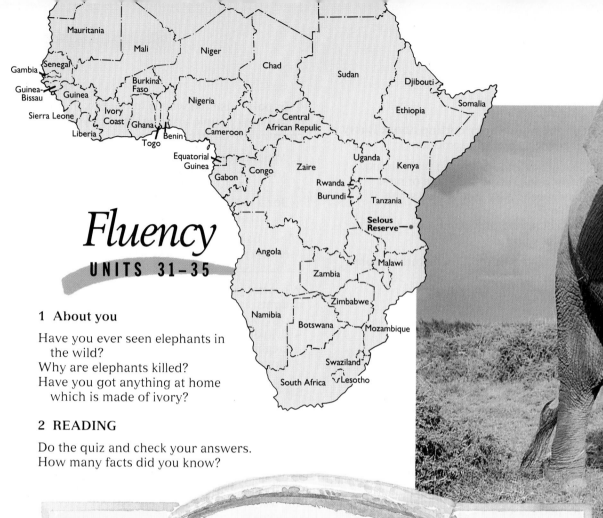

Fluency

UNITS 31–35

1 About you

Have you ever seen elephants in the wild?
Why are elephants killed?
Have you got anything at home which is made of ivory?

2 READING

Do the quiz and check your answers.
How many facts did you know?

Elephant Quiz

1 Ivory has many important uses. True or false?
False. Ivory is not used for anything important or useful. It is mostly used to make bracelets, chopsticks, handles for knives and forks and ornaments. In all cases, wood or plastic can be used instead.

2 An average-size ivory tusk is worth over £600. True or false?
True. In one country, there are stocks of ivory which are equivalent to the tusks of 70,000 elephants, and worth over £84 million.

3 Only tusks from fully-grown elephants are used. True or false?
False. There are so few fully-grown male elephants left that female and baby elephants are now also killed for their tusks. Tusks used in the ivory trade are now much smaller than they used to be – thirty centimetres long compared with two metres in the past.

4 Over the last ten years the elephant population has fallen by 25 per cent. True or false?
False. The elephant population has fallen by about 50 per cent during the last ten years. According to a recent report, one elephant is killed every ten minutes. If ivory poaching continues at this rate, there will be no elephants left in twenty-five years' time. One of the worst areas for poaching is the Selous Game Reserve in East Africa, where poachers move around in groups of twenty and use very sophisticated rifles.

5 All African countries want to have a ban on ivory trading. True or false?
False. A group of southern African countries, including Zimbabwe and Botswana, do not want a ban. They say that they produce their ivory by 'culling' – taking tusks only from weak or dying elephants. If there is a ban, they say they will ignore it.

3 Read all the information on these pages and make notes of the arguments for and the arguments against a ban on ivory trading. Try to think of three or four arguments on each side.

FOR A BAN   AGAINST A BAN
1 Ivory isn't
necessary in
our daily
lives.

4 Discussion

In groups of three or four, discuss whether you agree with a ban on ivory or not. Can you think of anything else that can be done to save the elephant?

5 WRITING

MR GEORGE MEDLEY, director of the World Wildlife Fund, said yesterday: 'We are asking every jeweller in every shop to remove ivory items from their windows today.'

Write the letter which you think Mr Medley sent to the jewellers. Use this guide:

Dear Sir,

I am director of . . . and I am writing to ask you . . .

You may not know the tragic facts about ivory poaching:
One elephant . . .
Even female . . .
Poachers . . .
The elephant population . . .
If . . . , there . . . . in twenty-five years' time.

Surely we do not want this to happen to the world's largest land mammal?

Yours faithfully,
. . .

◄Some of the most beautiful ornaments in the world are made from ivory.

▲'If there is a ban on ivory, many people will lose their jobs. Over 1200 people work in our ivory industry.'

▲ The money from one average-sized tusk will support a villager and his family for a year.

Check

1 Complete the sentences using the correct form of the verb *used to*.

used to   didn't use to   did . . . use to?

Example
1 When I was younger I . . . swimming once a week but I don't go at all now.
1 *When I was younger I used to go swimming once a week but I don't go at all now.*

1 When I was younger I . . . swimming once a week but I don't go at all now.
2 I . . . opera but I like it now.
3 My parents don't go out very much nowadays but they . . . a lot.
4 I know Terry smokes now but . . . before?
5 She . . . the piano beautifully but she doesn't play so well now.
6 . . . long hair or have you always had it short?

2 Match the two halves of the sentences, then rewrite them with *so . . . that*.

Example
1 I was tired   b) I fell asleep at the table.
1 *I was so tired that I fell asleep at the table.*

1 I was tired   a) we didn't have enough
2 He spoke quietly   money to pay for it.
3 The meal was   b) I fell asleep at the table.
  expensive   c) he became ill.
4 The book was   d) I took a whole roll of
  good   film.
5 The view was   e) nobody could hear him.
  spectacular   f) I finished it in one
6 He worked hard   evening.

3 Complete the sentences with *so* or *such a*.

Example
1 I've never seen . . . many people!
1 *I've never seen so many people!*

1 I've never seen . . . many people.
2 She's got . . . wonderful voice!
3 The play was . . . good that I want to see it again.
4 It's . . . small room I can hardly move in it!
5 He's made . . . much money that he doesn't need to work any more.
6 It was . . . lovely day that we took a picnic with us.

4 Complete the sentences with the correct verb form.

Example
1 If the phone (ring), I (answer) it.
1 *If the phone rings, I'll answer it.*

1 If the phone (ring), I (answer) it.
2 I (go) if you (want) me to.
3 you (be) all right if I (leave) you alone?
4 She (not be) pleased if you (not come).
5 If John (not arrive) soon, he (miss) the train.
6 he (be) angry if she (get) home late?

5 Rewrite the sentences choosing the correct verb tense.

Example
1 By the time I got to the café, it shut/had shut.
1 *By the time I got to the café, it had shut.*

1 By the time I got to the café, it shut/had shut.
2 I was very hungry because I haven't eaten/hadn't eaten any breakfast.
3 When I opened the door, the cat had run out/ran out.
4 When I arrived, I realised my mistake. I have got/had got the wrong day.
5 When she saw/had seen her present, she started to cry.
6 She ran downstairs to open the door but it was too late. The postman went/had gone.

6 An employer is explaining about interviews. Rewrite the instructions in the passive.

Example
1 'First we send you a letter inviting you to an interview.'
1 First you are sent a letter inviting you to an interview.

1 'First we send you a letter inviting you to an interview.'
2 'We pay for your return ticket.'
Your . . .
3 'We meet you at the station and take you to our office.'
You . . .
4 'We ask you to talk about yourself for a few minutes.'
You . . .
5 'After the interview we give you lunch.'
After . . . you . . .
6 'We tell you the result the next day.'
You . . .

7 Complete the sentences with the correct preposition.

to (×2)   for (×2)   from (×2)   by
of   in   with

Example
1 They sent him to prison.

1 They sent him . . . prison.
2 They banned him . . . driving.
3 The dogs are trained . . . two stages.
4 He was punished . . . smoking.
5 She was found guilty . . . stealing stamps . . . her office.
6 She was fined £12 . . . parking on the pavement.
7 They washed their clothes . . . hand.
8 It is covered . . . a fine powder.
9 I got home at six. . . . my surprise nobody was there.

8 Note the stress in these phrases.

Example
1 a fax machine
1 a FAX machINE

1 a fax machine
2 a washing machine
3 a driving test
4 a scuba diver
5 a weight belt
6 a prison sentence
7 a customs officer
8 a drug smuggler

9 Find at least eight words to do with CRIME in this word square. You can go across and down.

```
G A M P O L I C E A
U X W R Y C N M L R
I R F I N L J P T R
L Y G S M U G G L E
T O Z O S E O B Y S
Y Q I N N O C E N T
M C D R W Q I F X P
P U N I S H F I P N
B I A N P T K N E W
S U S P E C T E M Z
```

CHECK YOUR PROGRESS

Add up your score. How well did you do?

Problem exercises . . .

LEARNING TO LEARN 7: Checking yourself

Teachers do not always have time in class to check everything you say and write, so it is a good idea to learn to check yourself. Here are some ways to help you:

1 Think before you speak or write. A second of 'thinking time' can help you choose the correct tense or word.
2 Record yourself when you speak and listen to yourself later. Did you notice any mistakes?
3 When you do roleplays, make a note of anything you say which you think is wrong. Ask your teacher afterwards.
4 Check your written work for mistakes which you know you often make, e.g. the use of the future tenses, the continuous tenses, articles, etc.

Preview

⏹ **Match the text with the photographs. Then listen and see if you were right.**

| **A** He asked her what sort of car she was looking for. | **B** You said you were good at tennis! | **C** Are you romantic and emotional or practical and efficient? |

In Units 36–40 you will learn how to:

- report statements
- describe people's personalities
- report questions
- talk about fear and other emotions
- use some phrasal verbs

D You aren't afraid of flying, are you?

E I want you to cut it off. All of it!

114

Heartsearch

If you would like
a love story of your own
and want to find
that special person,
contact

Heartsearch,
14, Mill Street,
Romford,
Essex
Tel: 0708 01414

Heartsearch *One of the world's largest dating agencies*

-36-
Reported statements

Before you listen

What are dating agencies?
How do they try to match the right people?

1 ▭ DIALOGUE

'Heartsearch', a dating agency, arranged a date for Clare's friend, Ruth, and sent her a description of the man. After meeting him, Ruth telephoned the agency the next day.

RUTH: This is Ruth Talbot here. I'm telephoning about my date last night.
WOMAN: Oh yes, did you have a pleasant evening?
RUTH: No, it was a disaster. In fact, I'm rather confused!
WOMAN: Oh?
RUTH: Well, there are four things. Firstly, you said he was twenty-six but he's at least thirty-five.
WOMAN: Oh?
RUTH: I definitely said on my application form that I wanted to meet someone in their twenties.
WOMAN: Yes, I remember.
RUTH: Secondly, and this is rather strange, you said he had dark hair and brown eyes but in fact he has red hair and blue eyes.
WOMAN: Oh?
RUTH: And thirdly, you said he lived in Oxford but he doesn't. He lives in Bristol! That's too far away for me.
WOMAN: I'm sure that can't be right.
RUTH: And fourthly, you said he was interested in music and the theatre but he isn't. He's only interested in sport! In fact, he was really boring.
WOMAN: Just a moment. Was his name John Manning?
RUTH: No, it was Neil Carter.
WOMAN: Ah, that explains it. We sent you the wrong person. I'm so sorry, Miss Talbot!
RUTH: So am I!

Listen and choose the right answer.

1 Ruth telephoned the agency because
   a) the man did not arrive for her date.
   b) the man was too young for her.
   c) the man did not match the description.

2 The agency
   a) had not read Ruth's application form carefully.
   b) had sent the wrong person by mistake.
   c) had forgotten to tell John Manning that he had a date.

2 Complete the information about the two men.

Name:	John Manning	Neil Carter
Home town:	. . .	. . .
Age:	. . .	. . .
Appearance:	. . .	. . .
Interests:	. . .	. . .

GRAMMAR FOCUS: Reported statements

In reported speech, verbs in the present usually change to a form of the past, e.g.
am/is – was, live – lived, have/has – had, do – did.

Direct statement	Reported statement
'I'm thirty-five.'	He said (that) **he was** thirty-five.
'I want to go home.'	She said (that) **she wanted** to go home.
'I'm working this evening.'	He said (that) **he was working** this/that evening.
'I've been here before.'	She said (that) **she had been** here/there before.

Verbs in the past simple usually change to the past perfect tense.

'I met him a year ago.'	She said (that) **she had met** him a year ago.

Note
The use of *that* is optional.

3 What were the woman's original words to Ruth about John Manning?

1 'He's twenty-six.'

4 Report what Ruth said about herself to the agency.

1 She said (that) she was twenty-four.

1 'I'm twenty-four.'
2 'I live in a flat in Oxford.'
3 'I'm looking for a man in his twenties.'
4 'I want to meet someone interesting.'
5 'I'm keen on classical music.'
6 'I haven't got a car.'

5 ▣ SPEECHWORK

Has the word *that* a weak stress or a strong stress in the sentences? Listen and see if you were right.

1 That's my house.
2 She said that she was married.
3 Did she really say that?
4 He said that that was his best performance so far.
5 That's the company that John works for.

6 ▣ LISTENING

Josh has recently received a cassette letter from his friend, Gary, who is in La Paz, Bolivia. Read what Josh thinks is true. Then listen to the cassette and correct the facts.

Josh thinks that:
1 Gary has been in La Paz for a few weeks.
2 La Paz is the same altitude as Caracas.
3 it is always hot in La Paz.
4 Gary is staying in a company flat.
5 he has been to Peru before.
6 he is coming back to Britain in two months' time.

1 No. Gary said he had been in La Paz for two months.

116

-37-
Personality

1 READING

What star sign are you? Read the chart and find out about yourself.

2 VOCABULARY

Choose a word to match the definitions.

> brave loyal stubborn thoughtful
> selfish serious generous fussy tidy
> optimistic jealous honest

1 Someone who always remembers your birthday. (thoughtful)

Someone who:
1 always remembers your birthday.
2 is unwilling to change her/his mind.
3 worries too much about details.
4 only thinks about her/himself.
5 always tells the truth.
6 always supports her/his friends.
7 is not frightened of anything.
8 likes to keep things in their correct place.
9 doesn't laugh or make jokes very often.
10 wants what other people have got.
11 always believes good things will happen.
12 likes to give money, help or presents.

GRAMMAR FOCUS: Adverbs of degree

Adverbs of degree are used to modify adjectives.

I'm **very** stubborn.
I'm **rather** shy.
I'm **quite/fairly** shy.
I'm **a bit** selfish.
I'm **not at all** romantic.

Note
Some adverbs of degree are stronger than *very*, e.g. She's **terribly** kind. He's **awfully** stubborn. She's **extremely** selfish.

What's the difference in meaning?
1 The film was terribly good.
2 The film was terrible.

STAR SIGN	COLOUR	QUALITIES
CAPRICORN 22 Dec–19 Jan	pink blue	kind patient shy
AQUARIUS 20 Jan–18 Feb	orange blue	loyal kind stubborn
PISCES 19 Feb–20 Mar	green pink	artistic creative careless
ARIES 21 Mar–19 Apr	red brown	brave honest serious
TAURUS 20 Apr–20 May	green pale blue	reliable practical bossy
GEMINI 21 May–20 Jun	yellow purple	lively intelligent selfish
CANCER 21 Jun–22 Jul	grey green	romantic thoughtful moody
LEO 23 Jul–22 Aug	orange gold	happy generous emotional
VIRGO 23 Aug–22 Sep	black navy blue	hard-working tidy fussy
LIBRA 23 Sep–22 Oct	blue pink	easy-going optimistic greedy
SCORPIO 23 Oct–21 Nov	dark red white	imaginative enthusiastic jealous
SAGITTARIUS 21 Nov–21 Dec	red purple	relaxed generous careless

HOLIDAY ROMEOS

 **THE AMOROUS AUSTRALIAN**

He's called Barry. He's a bit scruffy but cheerful, great fun but completely broke! He's travelling around Europe with a group of friends and he's looking for a good time. He loves the beach, swims like a fish, drinks lager like water, never sunbathes but has a perfect tan. He's not a romantic but deep down, he's a nice chap. And if you're looking for lots of laughs–he's your man.

Romance rating:

 THE AMERICAN DREAMBOAT

He's called Chuck or Brent and he's 'doing' Europe. Not cheaply, like Barry from Australia, but with much more money and a tour guide to direct him and his group from famous sight to famous sight, and from coach to coach. He thinks your accent is 'cute'. He's terribly friendly. He'll tell you his whole life story by the end of Day One, and he'll be hurt if he doesn't know yours. He's generous and loves shopping. He's enthusiastic and embarrassingly honest. He's fun but don't expect him to stay for long. He's got a lot of sights to see.

Romance rating:

3

Find all the people who have the same star sign as you. Say if you are typical of your sign or not.

A: I think I'm quite shy and I'm fairly patient.
B: I don't think I'm shy but I'm quite patient.

Note

You say *I **don't think** I'm shy.* **not** I think I'm not shy.

4 WRITING

Use the notes and the ratings to compare Lisa's personality with her sister's.

LISA	HER SISTER
✓✓ emotional	✗✗ emotional
✓✓✓ untidy	✓✓ tidy
✗✗ shy	✓✓✓ shy
✓ easygoing	✗ serious

✗ rather	✗✗ not at all	✓ fairly
✓✓ very	✓✓✓ extremely	

Lisa is very emotional, whereas her sister is . . .

Now write sentences comparing two people in your family.

5 READING

Read the article and answer the questions.

1 Where do you think the article comes from?
2 What time of year do you think it appeared?
3 Is it serious?

6

Read the text and match the two people with two people in the illustration. What nationalities do you think the other types represent?

7 Find words in the text which mean:

1 very untidy
2 doesn't have any money
3 charming and attractive
4 upset and unhappy about something

8 About you

Have you ever met anybody who matched these stereotypes? Do you think they are funny or unfair?

118

-38-
Reported questions

💻 DIALOGUE

The police have stopped Clare
just outside Oxford.

CLARE: What's the matter? I wasn't driving
 too fast, was I?
OFFICER: No, it's all right. Just a few
 questions, madam, if you don't
 mind. Where are you going?
CLARE: Home. To Oxford.
OFFICER: And are you the owner of this car?
CLARE: Of course I am!
OFFICER: And where have you come from?
CLARE: London.
OFFICER: Do you work in London, madam?
CLARE: Yes, I do.
OFFICER: When did you last buy petrol?
CLARE: This morning on my way to work.
OFFICER: I see. And how long have you had
 this car?
CLARE: Oh, about a year. What's the
 problem?
OFFICER: There's been some trouble on the
 motorway. A hold-up at a service
 station, actually. A car just like this
 one was stolen.

1 Listen and choose the right answer.

1 The police stopped Clare because
 a) she was driving too fast.
 b) they wanted to check her car.
 c) she was driving a stolen car.

2 The police officer wanted to know
 a) if she owned the car.
 b) how long she had had her driving
 licence.
 c) where she worked in London.

3 The police officer said there had been
 a) an accident on the motorway.
 b) a traffic jam.
 c) a robbery.

**2 Report the questions which the police
officer asked Clare.**

1 He asked where she was going.

GRAMMAR FOCUS: Reported questions

In reported questions the word order of the question always changes.

Direct question	**Reported question**
He asked, 'What **are you** doing?'	He asked me what **I was** doing.

If there is no question word (*where, how, when,* etc.) in the question, *if* is used instead.

| 'Are you English?' | He asked **if** I was English. |

Do/does/did are not used in reported questions.

| 'Do you live in London?' | He asked if I lived in London. |

119

3 🔲 READING

Read the extract from a short story and answer the questions.

1 Why did Mary Maloney want to kill her husband?
2 How did she kill him?
3 Did she go to the grocer's before or after she killed him?
4 What did she tell the police had happened?
5 What do you think she decided to do with the leg of lamb? Why?

4 ROLEPLAY

Look at the paragraph beginning: 'They asked her questions.' Use the reported questions in the text to roleplay the conversation between one of the policemen and Mary.

5 WRITING

Write the next paragraph of the story in approximately 80–100 words.

6 🔲 LISTENING

Listen to an interview with an English crime writer who lives in the south of France. Complete the article.

Last week I interviewed John Cameron, the crime writer, in his new home in Antibes in the south of France. I asked him how many books . . . and he confessed that so far he . . . a single one. Too much of the good life? I asked . . . happy and he said . . . He said he . . . always . . . France. When asked what . . . about Britain, to my surprise, he mentioned the rain! I was interested to know . . . family and friends . . . Apparently he has non-stop visitors.

The Leg of Lamb

Mary Maloney loved her husband, Patrick, very much. She was going to have a baby and every day she looked forward to Patrick coming home from his job as a detective. Everything was perfect, until one evening he suddenly told her that he wanted to leave her. Mary was shocked and, as if in a dream, went to the freezer and took out a frozen leg of lamb for their supper.

A few minutes later, it was over. All right, she told herself, so I've killed him. She began to think very fast. She carried the meat to the kitchen, put it in a pan, turned the oven on, and put the pan inside. Then she washed her hands and ran upstairs to her bedroom. She sat down in front of the mirror, tidied her hair and tried to smile.

"I want some potatoes, please, Sam. Yes, and perhaps some beans."

She practised several times. Then she ran downstairs, went out of the back door and into the street. She went straight to the shop.

When she returned, she phoned the police.

"Quick! Come quickly! Patrick's dead!"

"Who's speaking?"

"Mrs Maloney. Mrs Patrick Maloney."

The car came very quickly, and when she opened the front door, two policemen walked in.

"Is he dead?" she cried.

"I'm afraid he is. What happened?"

They asked her questions. In a few words she told them what time Patrick had come home, what she was doing at the time, why she had gone to the grocer's, which grocer's she had gone to, what she had bought and how long she had spent there. She told them how she had put the meat into the oven – "It's there now" – before she left for the grocer's, and how she had come back to find him lying on the floor.

They left her there while they searched the house. They were looking for the murder weapon. "It's the old story," said Detective Noonan. "Get the weapon, and you've got the murderer . . ."

After searching the house, the policemen returned. "Do you know that your oven is still on, and the meat is still inside?"

"Oh," she said. "So it is." And she knew exactly what she was going to do . . .

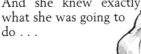

LIVING WITH FEAR

As the chief BBC news correspondent, Kate Adie has been in some very frightening situations. She has reported earthquakes in Armenia, fighting in the Middle East, floods in Bangladesh and events in China. She has been close to death a number of times. How does she cope with difficult situations?

' You can't stand there crying. My job is to report, not to break down in tears. But you have to be sensitive. I've heard people in total despair, and it's a noise unlike any other. It is the most awful sound, and I would not put it on television.'

'Brave reporters are dead reporters'

When American planes bombed the Libyan capital of Tripoli, Kate woke up and went out on to the balcony of her hotel. She saw the planes and the explosions, went back into her room and very carefully put on her earrings. 'It was a count-to-ten reaction,' she says.

Kate has learnt how degrading real fear can be. 'I think real fear is when you reach a point when you will do absolutely anything to get out of a situation you are in. Many people think you have to be very brave to do my job. But it's not true. Brave reporters are dead reporters. It is not my job to go into the fighting. I hide under the table like anyone else. When people say they would like to do my job, I ask them: "Are you prepared to be very very frightened?" '

1 READING

Read and guess the meaning.

correspondent   cope
break down in tears
sensitive   despair
degrading

Use the text to make the interviewer's questions for these answers.

1 I'm the chief news correspondent for the BBC.
2 Yes, I have. A number of times.
3 I was asleep in my hotel.
4 Because it was a 'count-to-ten reaction'.
5 Reaching a point where you will do absolutely anything to get out of the situation you are in.
6 No, you don't. Brave reporters are dead reporters.

2 What do you think?

What is a 'count-to-ten' reaction?
In what other situations can this be a useful reaction?

3 VOCABULARY

Find nouns in the text which are linked with the following verbs and adjectives.

1 die – death

1 die   2 noisy   3 explode
4 react   5 afraid

GRAMMAR FOCUS
Adjectives and prepositions

Many adjectives are followed by specific prepositions.

of
I'm **frightened/afraid of** the dark.
I'm **proud/ashamed of** what I did.

about
I'm **angry/annoyed/upset about** breaking the glass.
I'm **worried about** Jenny.

with
I'm **pleased/disappointed with** my exam results.
I'm **bored/fed up with** this book.
I'm **angry/annoyed with** her.

at
I'm **surprised/shocked at** the news.
I'm **good/bad/hopeless at** cooking.

Match these adjectives with a similar adjective in the list above.
1 terrified 2 amazed 3 delighted 4 nervous

Note
Words connected with *fear*. There are two adjectives *frightened* and *frightening* and a verb *to frighten*, e.g. *The film was **frightening**. I was **frightened**. The film **frightened** me.*

---

4 Write a sentence of your own for each of the following adjectives, using a suitable preposition.

worried   amazed   angry   nervous   terrified

5 🔲 LISTENING DIALOGUE

Complete Clare's telephone conversation with her mother, using the correct adjectives and prepositions from the Focus box.

ANN: Hello, it's me. You haven't phoned me for weeks. I was getting a bit . . . you.
CLARE: Sorry, Mum. I'm fine. In fact, I'm feeling very . . , myself at the moment.
ANN: Proud? Why?
CLARE: I had my first scuba-diving lesson last week.
ANN: Weren't you . . . being under water?
CLARE: Yes, I was absolutely terrified at first. But then I was O.K. In fact I'm quite . . . myself.
ANN: Do you think you're going to be . . . it?
CLARE: I hope so.
ANN: Good. Well, I'm glad you weren't . . . your first lesson.
CLARE: Disappointed? No, it was a great experience.
ANN: Anyway, I'm pleased to hear you're well. I'll speak to you again soon. Bye!

Now listen and see if you were right.

PHOBIA FACTS

About one in ten people suffer from special fears or 'phobias'.
The five most common are:

1 *arachnophobia* - fear of spiders
2 *aerophobia* - fear of flying
3 *agoraphobia* - fear of open spaces
4 *claustrophobia* - fear of being enclosed in a small space
5 *social phobia* - fear of meeting new people

6 In groups, use the 'phobia' list above to find out what frightens people most.

A: Are you frightened of spiders?
B: No, I'm not.
A: What about flying?
B: Yes, I'm afraid of flying sometimes.
A: Is there anything else you're frightened of?
B: Yes, I'm frightened of rats/snakes.

DOCTOR: So what's the problem?
SEAGULL: I'm afraid of flying.

122

The Gift

One dollar and eighty-seven cents. That was all. Three times Della counted it. And tomorrow was Christmas. She sat down on the old sofa and burst into tears. She had saved every penny for months and this was the result. Twenty dollars a week doesn't go far. Only $1.87 to buy a present for Jim. Her Jim. She had spent hours planning to buy something nice for him.

She went to the mirror and let down her hair. She let it fall to its full length, below her knees.

There were two possessions of which the Dillinghams were very proud. One was Jim's gold watch, which had been his grandfather's. The other was Della's hair.

She put her hair up again nervously and cried a little again. Then she put on her old brown jacket, her old brown hat and went down the stairs to the street.

She stopped at a sign which read: 'Madame Sofronie. Hair Goods of All Kinds'. She ran up the stairs.
'Will you buy my hair?' asked Della.
'Take your hat off,' said Madame Sofronie, 'and let me look at it.'
She let her hair down.
'Twenty dollars,' said Madame.
'Give it to me quickly,' said Della and the woman began to cut off Della's beautiful long hair.

For the next two hours Della searched for a present for Jim. Then she found it. It was a platinum chain for Jim's watch. As soon as she saw it, she knew it was right for Jim. It was like him. Quiet and valuable. It cost $21.

When Della got home, she started to curl her hair. After half an hour, her head was covered in small curls.

At seven o'clock the front door opened and Jim came in. Della whispered to herself: 'Please God, make him think I am still pretty.' Jim looked thin and serious. Poor Jim! He was only twenty-two! His eyes fixed upon Della and there was an expression on his face which frightened her.
'Jim, darling, don't look at me like that. My hair will grow again. I cut it off and sold it because I wanted to buy you a present. I've got a beautiful present for you.'
'You've cut off your hair,' said Jim slowly.
'Yes, but I'm still me without my hair, aren't I?'
'Your hair is gone,' he said again, almost like an idiot.
He took a package from his coat pocket and threw it on the table. Della tore at the string and paper. First, an ecstatic scream. Then, hysterical tears.

For there lay the combs – the set of beautiful, tortoiseshell hair combs which she had wanted for so long. She knew they were expensive.
She hugged them closely and said: 'My hair grows very fast, Jim.'
Then she jumped up and gave him her present. The platinum watchchain flashed in the light.
'Isn't it beautiful, Jim? Give me your watch. I want to see how it looks on it.'

Jim sat down on the sofa and smiled. 'Dell,' he said, 'let's put our Christmas presents away and keep them for a while. They're too nice to use at present. I sold the watch to buy your combs. Now let's have supper.'

The wise men invented the art of giving Christmas presents. This was the story of two foolish young people who sacrificed for each other their most important possessions. But of all who give presents, these two were the wisest.

-40-
Short story

Before you read

When do people give each other presents?
What is the story going to be about?

1 ▣ READING

Read the story and answer the questions.

1 What two possessions did Della and Jim Dillingham value most highly?
2 How much did Della have to spend on a Christmas present for Jim?
3 How did she manage to buy him a present?
4 What did she buy for Jim?
5 What did Jim buy for her?
6 How did he get the money to buy it?

2 Read and think.

1 How long ago do you think the story took place? Why?
2 How do you know that the Dillinghams were poor?
3 How long do you think they had been married?
4 Do you think the Dillinghams were happy?

GRAMMAR FOCUS: Phrasal verbs

Verbs are often used together with prepositions like *on, off, in, out, at, for, up, down*. These are called phrasal verbs. Some phrasal verbs can take an object. When the object is a noun it can go in two places, either before the preposition or after it.

1 She let **her hair** down.
2 She let down **her hair**.

However, when the object is a pronoun, it can only go before the preposition, e.g. *She let **it** down.* **not** She let down it.

Find five more examples in the text of phrasal verbs which take an object. Look for the following verbs:

put   take   cut

What different prepositions are used?

3 Answer the questions using one of the phrasal verbs in the box.

put down   put on   put up   take off

1 What do people with long hair sometimes do to their hair when they play sport?
2 What do you say to a child who has just picked up a piece of broken glass?
3 What do you do when you go out in cold weather?
4 What do you do with an anorak when you come into a warm house?
5 What do you do with a tent when you want to sleep in it?

4 ▣ SPEECHWORK

Which word is stressed in each sentence? Listen and see if you were right.

Put it down! Take it off! Put them on!
Tell Simon to put down the glass.
Why don't you take off your coat?
I'm going to put on my boots.

Now listen and repeat the sentences.

5 VOCABULARY

When telling a dramatic story, it is common to choose colourful rather than ordinary words, e.g. *wonderful* instead of *nice*, *brilliant* instead of *good*.

Find words in the text that have a similar meaning to the following but are more dramatic and colourful.

1 started to cry
2 put it (on the table)
3 opened (the package)
4 very happy
5 uncontrolled
6 held them to her closely
7 got up
8 shone

6 ▣ LISTENING

Listen to John describing a story he has just read and answer the questions.

1 What did the friend borrow?
2 What happened to it?
3 What did the friend do?
4 Why was this a mistake?

124

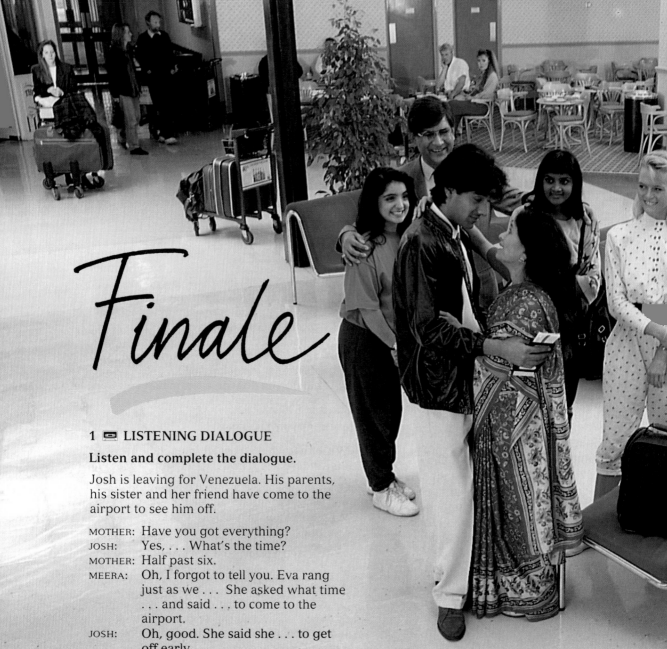

Finale

1 🔊 LISTENING DIALOGUE

Listen and complete the dialogue.

Josh is leaving for Venezuela. His parents, his sister and her friend have come to the airport to see him off.

MOTHER: Have you got everything?
JOSH: Yes, . . . What's the time?
MOTHER: Half past six.
MEERA: Oh, I forgot to tell you. Eva rang just as we . . . She asked what time . . . and said . . . to come to the airport.
JOSH: Oh, good. She said she . . . to get off early.
FATHER: Well, she'll have to hurry.
MEERA: By the way, Josh, . . . your Walkman while you're away?
JOSH: O.K. But don't break it! Ah, there's Eva.
EVA: Josh! I thought perhaps you . . . !
JOSH: Almost but not quite!
EVA: I hate . . .
JOSH: Don't say that! It's not for long. Promise . . .
EVA: I'll write . . . !
FATHER: Come on, Josh. Time to go.
MOTHER: . . .
MEERA: Be good!
JOSH: Why?
MOTHER: Josh!
JOSH: . . . Bye Mum, Dad, Meera. Bye Eva. Take care!

2 Complete the summary of the dialogue with the past simple, past continuous or past perfect simple tense of the verbs in brackets.

Josh (go) to the airport with his parents and his sister, Meera. While they (wait) at the airport, Meera suddenly (remember) that she (have) something important to tell Josh. Eva (phone) just as they (leave) to ask what time Josh's flight (leave). Previously Eva (think) that she wouldn't be able to get to the airport in time but in fact, she (turn) up while Josh (say) goodbye to his parents. He finally (go through) passport control and everyone (wave) goodbye.

125

8, South Street,
Double Bay,
Sydney,
N.S.W. 2028,
Australia,
2nd October

Dear Clare,

Well, here I am finally back home. I really can't believe that I've been so far across the world. Unfortunately, the flight wasn't very good. We were delayed in Singapore for five hours, so I was very glad to have the Walkman you gave me. Also, I had already seen the in-flight movie in Oxford.

Anyway, thank you again for letting me stay with you for such a long time. It was really kind of you. I had a wonderful time. I'm so pleased I managed to visit Scotland and Ireland as well.

Mum and Dad hope I didn't cause you too much trouble! Of course they're really pleased to have me back. They gave me this typewriter as a homecoming present!

They want you to come over and visit them soon. Would you like to come? I know you're busy but you'd love it here in Australia. What about planning a trip in the New Year? Think about it and let us know.

Best wishes from all of us here. Give my regards to Bob, and Josh if you see him. I hope he enjoys Venezuela!

Lots of love,

Lisa

3 ROLEPLAY

A conversation at the international departure gate at an airport

STUDENT A
You are going to spend six months working in Canada as a tour guide. Your friend B comes to the airport to say goodbye. The flight to Canada will take over eight hours. You like flying very much, especially long distances. You are quite pleased to get away from home for a while. You are a keen letter-writer. Respond to B's conversation.

STUDENT B
You have gone to the airport to say goodbye to your friend A, who is going to work in Canada.
Ask how long the flight will take and if A is afraid of flying.
Tell A what you know about Canada and what Canadian people are like.
Ask when A is coming back.
Ask if you can use A's English books while he/she is away.
Wish A luck and tell him/her to write.

4 WRITING

When she got back to Australia, Lisa wrote to Clare to thank her.

Write a similar letter of thanks to some English friends you have been staying with.

Describe your flight and say if you enjoyed it or not.
Thank your friends for having you to stay and say how much you enjoyed staying with them.
Mention any trips you especially enjoyed.
Invite your friends back to your country.
Give your regards to your friends' parents or children.
End the letter with *Best wishes* or *Love* as you wish.

Check

1 A young man is being interviewed for a job as an au pair in New York. Report the questions and the answers.

Example
1 'How old are you?' 'I'm nineteen.'
1 *She asked him how old he was.*
He said he was nineteen.

1 'How old are you?' 'I'm nineteen.'
2 'How long are you staying?' 'I'm staying for three months.'
She asked him . . .
He said he . . . for three months.
3 'Have you got a driving licence?' 'Yes, I've had one for two years.'
She asked him . . . a driving licence.
He said he . . . for two years.
4 'What languages do you speak?' 'I speak French and Spanish.'
She asked him . . .
He said he . . . French and Spanish.
5 'What sports do you like?' 'I like baseball, tennis and swimming.'
She asked him . . .
He said he . . . baseball, tennis and swimming.
6 'Do you like children?' 'Yes, I like them very much.'
She asked him . . . children.
He said he . . . them very much.

2 Punctuate the paragraph. Use full stops (.), commas (,), question marks (?), apostrophes ('), capital letters and inverted commas (' ').

alice went in and walked towards the receptionist i have an appointment at ten oclock she said oh yes said the receptionist who had red hair and an irish accent could you sit over there alice sat down and looked at herself in the mirror she hadnt wanted to come at all then a girl who called herself kirsty asked her what she wanted id like you to cut it all off please

3 Choose the correct word to complete the sentences.

Example
1 He has lots of good ideas. He's very . . .
a) hard-working   (b) imaginative
c) thoughtful

1 He has lots of good ideas. He's very . . .
a) hard-working   b) imaginative
c) thoughtful
2 She never wears anything dirty or untidy. In fact she's very . . . about her clothes.
a) fussy   b) artistic   c) scruffy
3 He's very . . . He enjoys telling people what to do.
a) greedy   b) bossy   c) tidy
4 She was very . . . of all his past girlfriends.
a) stubborn   b) broke   c) jealous
5 You only think of yourself. You're so . . .
a) thoughtful   b) selfish   c) greedy
6 His clothes are always untidy. In fact he always looks very . . .
a) scruffy   b) shy   c) lively
7 Jenny has always given a lot of money to charity. She's very . . .
a) romantic   b) serious   c) generous
8 Sometimes she's happy. Sometimes she's sad. I've never known anyone so . . .
a) jealous   b) moody
c) embarrassing

4 Put the adverbs in order of their strength from 1 to 5.

a bit   extremely   very
not at all   fairly

Example
1 *not at all*

5 Complete the sentences using the correct preposition.

Example
1 Susie did very well in her exams. We're very proud . . . her.
1 *Susie did very well in her exams. We're very proud of her.*

1 Susie did very well in her exams. We're very proud . . . her.
2 You mean you haven't thanked them for your present yet? I'm ashamed . . . you.
3 I'm really disappointed . . . my new fax. It doesn't work very well.
4 I don't want to go up the Eiffel Tower. I'm terrified . . . heights.
5 I'm starting a new job next week. I'm very excited . . . it.
6 Bob isn't looking at all well. I'm very worried . . . him.
7 I'm extremely angry . . . my brother. He borrowed my alarm clock and broke it!
8 I'm bored . . . this exercise now. Let's stop!

6 Complete the sentences using *it, them* or *me* and the correct form of the phrasal verb.

turn on   take off   look up   wake up
put on   put up   try on   put down

Example
1 I'm too hot with this jacket on. Do you mind if I . . . ?
1 *I'm too hot with this jacket on. Do you mind if I take it off?*

1 I'm too hot with this jacket on. Do you mind if I . . . ?
2 I need to get up early tomorrow. Could you . . . at six o'clock?
3 I like these trousers. Can I . . . , please?
4 This is such an exciting book. I can't . . .
5 Here's a sweater. Why don't you . . . if you're cold?
6 I don't know that word. I'll . . . in a dictionary.
7 I'd like to watch the news on television. Can you . . . ?
8 My hair is so untidy. I think I'll . . . for the interview.

CHECK YOUR PROGRESS

Add up your score. How well did you do?

Problem exercises . . .

LEARNING TO LEARN 8: Language awareness

Try to be aware of the English language around you. Here are some ways to help you do this:

1 If you meet any English-speaking friends or visitors to your country, ask them questions. Find out how to say things and don't be afraid to ask them to speak more slowly. A useful phrase to remember is: 'Sorry I didn't catch that. Could you say it again, please?'
2 Listen to how English-speaking people speak and behave. Notice:
   – any conversational expressions they use often. Perhaps you could use some of these too, e.g. *Well, Anyway,* etc.
   – how they use their voices.
   – how they use their hands and bodies when they talk.
   – what sort of facial expressions they use.
3 Try to notice all examples of English around you, e.g. in advertisements, pop songs, notices, films, newspapers and magazines. Keep a notebook and write down new words which you think are useful or important.

Vocabulary and expressions

Some of the words listed below have already been introduced in Blueprint One.

Preview 1–5

agency
camp
director
employment
instructor
interview
leader
tour guide

get (a job)
help
hope
look for
stay

exciting
interested

abroad

part
studio
traffic

enjoy
go away
iron
mind
share
surprise
vacuum (clean)

bright (colour)
daily
helpful
untidy

actually
late
partly

saxophone
trumpet
vibration
violin

communicate
lip-read
miss (a turn)

deaf

Preview 6–10

luggage

spare

Unit 6

direction
end
garage
landmark
stadium
traffic lights
turning
way (the way to)

receive

along
around
as far as
down
into
past

You can't miss it.
You're welcome.

Unit 7

alcohol
asthma attack
booking
brandy
coach party
drama
duty
expert
fine
hairdresser
law
manager
military service
model (fashion)
needle
personal assistant
trip

breathe
carry
pay
sterilise

attractive
creative
efficient
hardworking
intelligent
local
patient
practical
reliable
resourceful
smart

all the time
on the spot
on your toes

Unit 1

ballet
festival
frankfurter
questionnaire
receptionist
stay

fill in
go well
look forward to

delicious
foreign

close

Nice to meet you.

Unit 2

accommodation
bike
change (of
  circumstance)
driving licence
experience
holiday village
information
knowledge
moped
officer
organisation
reason
secretary

apply (for a job)
hold (= have)
sound

enthusiastic
overseas

somewhere

a bit
as advertised
just
over (= more than)

Yours sincerely

Unit 3

designer
dishwasher
fashion show
household job
jet lag
laundry
noon

Unit 4

billion
fact
flood
habit
hero
luck
male
million
survey
team sport

attract
keep fit

astonishing
popular
recent

on sale

frequently
hardly ever
regularly

Unit 5

certificate
degree (university)
goldfish bowl
market town
night duty
resident
suburb
undergraduate

crowded
dreadful
ordinary
polluted
separate

everybody

nearly
nowadays

in fact
the same
the trouble is

Fluency 1–5

cheekbone
clarinet
composer
drum
musical instrument
musician
percussion

Unit 8

air conditioning
attention
brochure
code (dialling)
early morning call
entertainment
lift

borrow
bring
manage
turn on/off
use

Unit 9

au pair
conflict
consequence
convention
visit

chat
continue
decide
dream
emigrate
grab
miss
realise
shake
shrug (your
  shoulders)

homesick
lonely

angrily

anyone
nobody
no one

Reflexive pronouns
myself
yourself
(see complete list in
  Language review)

Unit 10

animal
battle
bagpipes
bird
bush
cliff
cloth
eagle
field
island
lake
last (the ...)
mountain
nation
New Year's Eve
path
pattern
per cent
plant
poet
rock
soldier
song
stone
stream

tartan
taste
tweed
valley
volcano
wilderness
whisky
wood (a ...)

cover
govern

criss-cross
empty
fresh
golden
major
rare
rocky
special
spectacular
untrue
wild
woollen

Fluency 6–10

blanket
guest

temporary

behind

Preview 11–15

crew
race
yacht

complete
erupt

Unit 11

camping site
choice
crossing
cure
diameter
half board
meeting
motorway
president
prime minister
resort
snack
towel

be able to
predict
promise
rent

twin-bedded (room)

approximately
at the bottom
once
urgently

Don't worry
Kind regards

Unit 12

alcoholic
ambition
cardboard box
chance
doorway

entrance
freedom
literature
opportunity
policy
rest (= remainder)
shelter
squat

beg
busk
earn
escape
estimate
regret
run out

degrading
homeless
permanent

all
a few
both
everybody
everyone
many
most
none
somebody
someone

almost

Unit 13

brain damage
folk dancing
idea
institute
reception
sheep
suggestion
treatment

disapprove
organise

similar

traditional
worried

Good luck!

Unit 14

baggage
emergency rations
flight
leg (of a race)
section
skipper (=captain)
tablet

compete
complain
delay
drop (of wind)
expect
land
pass
reach
rest
sail

depressed
pointed

already
at last
just

still
yet

if necessary
in sight of
probably

Unit 15

firefighter
flame
forest fire
holidaymaker
smoke
square

break out
breathe
burn
climb
cough
cry
destroy
put out
rescue
spread

frightened

in the distance

Fluency 11–15

current
dolphin
incident
item
reporter
sand
shark
shore
slogan
wave

attack
bite
charge
print
pull
push
raise
recover
save (someone's life)

Preview 16–20

pickpocket
rush hour
seat belt

during

Unit 16

advertisement
chat show
comedy
crime series
documentary
famine
food shortage
lorry
quantity
quiz show
soap opera
TV channel
violence

be annoyed with
    someone

political

not enough
too many
too much

in my opinion
on the whole

Unit 17

advice
beads
chewing gum
death
divorce
insomnia
lifestyle
nerve
pressure
relationship
remedy
sleeping pill
state
stress
tranquilliser
yoga

calm
cause
concentrate
get angry
hide
ought to
relax
relieve
result (in)
suffer (from)
take (medicine)

common
simple

especially

Unit 18

army
belief
boarding card
cathedral
cigar
crowd
culture
election
hand luggage
legal age
make-up
passenger
pension
permission
pipe
religion
rule
toilet

be allowed to
check in
own

devoted
sacred
silly
strict

eventually
(not) old enough

Unit 19

announcement
compartment
exhibition
high heels
mugger
palace
warning

avoid
carry
fasten
forget
keep something safe
knock
make sure
point
remember

shout
warn

confident
exaggerated
frightened
loud
royal
safe
secure
useful
weak

after dark
alone
in the dark

Be careful!
Look out!
Watch out!

Unit 20

art dealer
artist
climate
cornfield
ear
fit
gun
lifetime
madness
painting
preacher
sadness
sunflower
sunlight

be worth
cut off
die
kill
make friends (with)
shoot (a person)

colourful
contented
dull
energetic
junior (school)
mentally ill
miserable
religious
secondary (school)

finally

properly

at the age of

Reflexive pronoun
himself
(see complete list in
    Language review)

Fluency 16–20

area
document
embassy
research
tap water

hire
recommend
tip

suitable

Preview 21–25

aunt
bill
forecast
seaweed
storm

according to

Unit 21

binoculars
birdwatching
catastrophe
century
compass
disaster
drought
effect
environment
globe
grain
heatwave
hurricane
ice
iceberg
latitude
monsoon
region
scientist
sky

get (= become)
give (somebody a
    ring)
light (a fire)
melt
take (a photograph)

circular
global
lost
polar
surprising
tropical
violent

apparently
extremely
on record

Goodness!
How are things
    with ...?

Unit 22

ashtray
cigarette end
light
novel
rubbish

clear away
empty
take out
tidy

impatient
kind

I don't care
if not
if possible
if so

Unit 23

brand
caviare
experiment
fabric
frying pan
glass jar
image
jug
massage
memory
octopus
onion
packaging
product
rainbow
researcher
sauce

sausage
snake
sound effect
sunset
tap
tongue

advertise
associate
bake
claim
create
develop
excite
influence
last
percolate
pour
touch

Stative verbs
feel
look
seem
smell
sound
taste

appetizing
chlorinated
delicious
juicy
mouth-watering
purple
ripe
sensual
sizzling
unpleasant
unpopular

seriously

Unit 24

fireplace
mask
ornament
pipe
typewriter
vase
walking stick

turn up (at)

retired

Unit 25

aisle
choice
cockpit
hijack(er)
jumbo jet
nightmare
ordeal
pilot
prayer
priest
request
side
vacancy

appear
comfort
disappear
go through (an
    experience)
scream
see someone about
    something
serve
shut up (= be quiet)
surrender
work (= be
    successful)

anxious
disappointed
frustrated
nasty
responsible
terrible
upset
wonderful

anyway

Fluency 21–25

alien
buzz
candle
circle
crop
hedgehog
helicopter
hoax
mystery
spaceship
theory
tractor
whirlwind
witness

cause
examine
vary

satisfactory
sensible

Preview 25–30

tandem

envious

surprised

Unit 26

boxing
cattle
engine
genius
golf
power
sensation
status
victory

believe in
crash
motivate

arrogant
excellent
impossible
private

Unit 27

attic
freestyle
hole
scheme
seat
steward
straw
symphony
tray
unrest

cancel
hang
joke
knock
shatter
sink
suck
throw away

priceless
short of (something)

miraculously

narrowly
safely

Good heavens!
in aid of
No, really!
What a surprise!
You're joking!

Unit 28

accent
monument
wildlife

bring up
collect

comfortable
elegant
impressive
strong (accent)
several
tiring
unusual
useless

definitely

Unit 29

attitude
business
check (Am.E) (= bill)
choice of food
cost of living
impression
pace of life
portion
standard of living

compulsory

generally

as for
for example
when it comes to

Unit 30

aborigine
condition
desert
exploitation
inhabitant
kangaroo
settler
stage

build
fight
protect
survive

encouraging
original
remote

softly

Fluency 26–30

adventure
airfare
engagement
gift
personality
talent
vegetarian

announce

brilliant

Preview 31–35

block (office ...)
emerald
stage (theatre)
wetsuit

Unit 31

accounts
central heating
deep freeze
dishwasher
fax machine
microwave
vacuum cleaner
washing machine

celebrate
integrate
interpret
sweep
tease

depressing
worthwhile

by hand

Unit 32

atmosphere
electricity
elephant
paradise
result
roll (of film)
seal (= animal)
video screen

faint
fall asleep
fly away
queue

amazing
crazy
fantastic
primitive
trumpeting

Unit 33

arrangement
breath
driving test
equipment
flippers
lungs
outing
surface
weight belt

dive
get on with
   something
hold
mist up
rinse out
threaten

painful

correctly
each other

Unit 34

beard
earthquake
fairy-tale
ground
moment
piece
romance
wedding

crack
creep
delay
get through to
   someone
recognise
shake
shave
sway
tremble
turn up

to my great relief

Unit 35

aid
bloodstain
crime
criminal
drug
explosive
fingerprint
laboratory
reward
sample
sticky tape
strand
surface
suspect

ban
catch someone doing
   something
compare
detect
fine
hide
lift
place
search
send to prison
smuggle
sniff
solve
steal
train

fine (= thin)
genetic
unique
visible

out of sight

Fluency 31–35

bracelet
chopstick
equivalent
fork
game reserve
handle
ivory
jeweller
mammal
plastic
rifle
tusk

poach
stock
trade

fully-grown
sophisticated
tragic

Preview 36–40

emotional
romantic

Unit 36

altitude
dating agency

match

confused

at least
in their twenties

Unit 37

star sign
stereotype
(tourist) sight
type

amorous
bossy
broke (coll.)
cute (coll.)
easy-going
embarrassing(ly)
funny
fussy
generous
greedy
honest
imaginative
jealous
moody
optimistic
selfish
serious
scruffy
shy
stubborn
thoughtful
tidy

fairly
rather
whereas

Unit 38

grocer's
hold-up
lamb
oven
owner
pan
robbery
weapon

confess
mention
search
shock

frozen
non-stop

Unit 39

balcony
correspondent
earring
explosion
fear
rat
reaction
seagull
situation
spider

bomb
break down
cope with
frighten
get out of

amazed (at)
annoyed (about)
ashamed (of)
delighted (with)
fed up (with)
frightening
glad
hopeless (at)
proud (of)
sensitive (about)
shocked (at)
terrified (of)

absolutely

in tears

Unit 40

anorak
chain
curl
expression (facial)
hair comb
idiot
package
platinum
tent
tortoiseshell

burst into tears
cut off
flash
hug
invent
jump
let down
put down
put on
put up
sacrifice
shine
value

ecstatic
hysterical
uncontrolled
wise

Finale

get off work
let somebody do
   something

previously

Give my regards to
Lots of love
Take care!

Language review

VERB TENSES

The following tenses are revised and expanded.

PRESENT SIMPLE (Units 1, 2, 3, 4, 5)

Positive	*Negative*	*Question*
I work here.	I don't work here.	Do I work here?
You/We/They work here.	You/We/They don't work here.	Do you/we/they work here?
He/She works here.	He/She doesn't work here.	Does he/she work here?

In this book, the present simple is used to:
- give personal details — *I live in Madrid.* (Units 1, 2)
- describe present situations — *He works in London.* (Unit 2)
- talk about likes and dislikes — *I like washing up.* (Unit 3)
- talk about routines — *I get up late.* (Units 3, 4)
- talk about frequency — *I hardly ever buy Newsweek.* (Unit 4)
- describe places — *The university has thirty-five colleges.* (Unit 5)

PAST SIMPLE (Units 1, 9, 20, 36, 38, 40)

Positive	*Negative*	*Question*
I worked here.	I didn't work here.	Did I work here?
You/We/They worked here.	You/We/They didn't work here.	Did you/we/they work here?
He/She worked here.	He/She didn't work here.	Did he/she work here?

In this book, the past simple is used to talk about:
- past events — *I went to the cinema last night.* (Unit 1)
- past consequences — *I was lonely so I joined a club.* (Units 9, 40)
- narrative events — *The teacher grabbed my pencil and shook his finger at me.* (Unit 9)
- biographical events — *He left Holland and joined his brother.* (Unit 20)
- historical events — *Van Gogh was born in Holland in 1853.* (Unit 20)
- reported statements — *You said (that) he lived in Oxford.* (Unit 36)
- reported questions — *He asked if I lived in London.* (Unit 38)

PRESENT CONTINUOUS (Units 1, 21)

Positive	*Negative*	*Question*
I'm working now.	I'm not working now.	Am I working now?
You/We/They're working now.	You/We/They aren't working now.	Are you/we/they working now?
He/She's working now.	He/She isn't working now.	Is he/she working now?

In this book, the present continuous is used to:
- express present activities — *I'm writing a letter.* (Unit 1)
- describe future arrangements — *She's going to Ireland next week.* (Unit 21)
- talk about temporary situations — *I'm staying with my German penfriend.* (Unit 1)

Some verbs are not normally used in the continuous tenses, e.g. *think, believe, understand, like, know, want, hear, see, smell, feel, sound, taste.* They are only used in the present continuous when they become deliberate, e.g. *What are you doing? I'm thinking.*

GOING TO FUTURE (Units 1, 21)

Positive	*Negative*	*Question*
I'm going to work tomorrow.	I'm not going to work tomorrow.	Am I going to work tomorrow?
You/We/They're going to work tomorrow.	You/We/They aren't going to work tomorrow.	Are you/we/they going to work tomorrow?
He/She's going to work tomorrow.	He/She isn't going to work tomorrow.	Is he/she going to work tomorrow?

In this book, the *going to* future is used to:
– talk about plans and future intention   *I'm going to stay at home this weekend.* (Unit 1)
– make predictions from present evidence   *We're going to have a lovely autumn.* (Unit 21)

VERB *HAVE GOT* (Units 1, 2)

Positive	*Negative*	*Question*
I've got a car.	I haven't got a car.	Have I got a car?
You/We/They've got a car.	You/We/They haven't got a car.	Have you/we/they got a car?
He/She's got a car.	He/She's got a car.	Has he/she got a car?

In this book, *have got* is used to talk about:
– family   *I've got two sisters and a brother.* (Unit 1)
– qualifications   *Have you got a driving licence?* (Unit 2)
– possessions   *I haven't got a car.* (Unit 2)

PRESENT PERFECT SIMPLE (Units 1, 2, 14)

Positive	*Negative*	*Question*
I've worked in France.	I haven't worked in France.	Have I worked in France?
You/We/They've worked in France.	You/We/They haven't worked in France.	Have you/we/they worked in France?
He/She's worked in France.	He/She hasn't worked in France.	Has he/she worked in France?

In this book the present perfect simple is used to:
– talk about experience   *I haven't been to Scotland but I've been to Ireland.* (Unit 1)
– talk about length of time up to the present with *for* and *since*   *How long have you lived there? I've lived there for five years/since 1988.* (Unit 2)
– talk about events which have happened recently with *just, already, still, yet*   *They've just arrived.* (Unit 14)
    I've already seen it. (Unit 14)

The following new tenses and structures are introduced.

PAST CONTINUOUS (Unit 15)

Positive			*Negative*			*Question*			*Short answer Positive*			*Short answer Negative*		
I	was	working.	I	wasn't	working.	Were	you	working?	Yes,	I	was.	No,	I	wasn't.
He			He				we							
She			She				they			we	were.		we	weren't.
										they			they	
We	were		We	weren't		Was	I			you	were.		you	weren't.
You			You				he							
They			They				she			he	was.		he	wasn't.
										she			she	

In this book the past continuous is used:
– in contrast with the past simple   *We were camping in France when forest fires broke out.*
– to describe events happening at a specific time   *What were you doing at ten o'clock last night?*
    I was having coffee with a friend.
– to give the background to events   *Some men were playing 'boules'.*
For a list of verbs which are not normally used in the continuous tenses, see the *present continuous* section of this Language review.

PAST PERFECT (Units 34, 36, 38)

Positive
I'd (had) gone.

Negative
I hadn't gone.

Question

Had I gone?

Short answer
Positive
Yes, you had.

Short answer
Negative
No, you hadn't.

In this book the past perfect is used:
- to describe an event which occurred before another in the past

When he arrived at the station, the train had left.   (Unit 34)

- in reported statements
- in reported questions

She said (that) she had met him a year ago.   (Unit 36)
They asked her why she had gone to the grocer's.   (Unit 38)

IMPERATIVE (Units 6, 19, 25)

Positive
Go past the church.

Negative
Don't worry.

In this book the imperative is used for:
- directions
- warnings and advice

- commands

Turn right at the bank.   (Unit 6)
Never take a lot of money with you.   (Unit 19)
Don't forget to lock your door.   (Unit 19)
Talk to Bob.   (Unit 25)
Don't phone me.   (Unit 25)

PASSIVE FORM (Unit 35)

Present simple passive

It is | made in Britain.
They are |

The passive is used when we are interested in the process or the events rather than the person who is/was responsible for them, e.g. *You are fined* is more common than *The police fine him* because we are not interested in who fines the person. It is formed by combining a tense of the verb *to be* with a past participle of the main verb.

In this book the passive is used to:
- describe processes
- talk about legal procedures with impersonal *you*

The dogs are trained in two stages.
You are sent to prison.

GERUND -*ING* FORM (Units 3, 20)

In this book the gerund or -*ing* form is used:
- after verbs like: *love, like, enjoy, don't mind, hate*

I like cooking./I don't mind cleaning.   (Unit 3)

- to express sequence of time with *before* and *after*

After leaving school, I went to university.   (Unit 20)
Before becoming a painter, he was a teacher.   (Unit 20)

With *before* and *after* + gerund, the subject must be the same in both clauses. (See the *time clauses in the past* section of this Language review.)

134

QUESTION TAGS (Units 26, 27)

With a positive sentence, you use a negative tag.   *He's late, isn't he?*
With a negative sentence, you use a positive tag.   *He isn't late, is he?*
The tag uses the auxiliary verbs, e.g. *is, are, was, were, have, can, do, does, did.*

1 In questions beginning with *I'm*, the negative tag is *aren't I*, e.g. *I'm late, aren't I?*
2 Question tags are often used in remarks about the weather, e.g. *It's a lovely day, isn't it?*

In this book question tags are used to:
– check and confirm facts   *He comes from Brazil, doesn't he?* (Unit 26)
    He isn't married, is he? (Unit 26)
– express surprise   *He wasn't, was he?* (Unit 27)

MODAL VERBS

The following modal verbs are used in this book:
can, could, shall, should, ought to, must, may, might, will, would, need

1 The form of the modal is the same with each pronoun, e.g. *I/you/he/they can't sing.*
2 Modals always come before the main verb in positive and negative sentences, e.g. *I must go.*
3 Questions are formed by inverting the subject and the modal, e.g. *Where shall we go?*
4 The negative is formed by putting *not* (*n't*) immediately after the modal verb, e.g. *I mustn't/couldn't/shouldn't.* The exception is the modals *will* (negative = *won't*) and *shall* (negative = *shan't*).
5 *Have to* is used instead of *must* in future and past tenses, e.g. *she'll have to, she had to.*

CAN (Units 6, 8, 22, 24)

In this book can is used to:
– express ability   (throughout)
– make requests   *Can I use the phone, please?* (Units 6, 8, 22)
– offer help   *Can I help you?* (Unit 8)
– refuse help   *I'm sorry. I'm afraid I can't.* (Unit 8)
– draw conclusions   *He can't be Italian.* (Unit 24)

The infinitive of *can* (ability) is *to be able to*, e.g. *If you go sailing, you must be able to swim.*

COULD (Units 8, 13, 22, 24)

In this book could is used to:
– make requests   *Could I have a brochure, please?* (Units 8, 22)
– make suggestions   *We could show her some folk dancing.* (Unit 13)
– draw conclusions   *He could be Spanish.* (Unit 24)

SHALL (Units 8, 13)

In this book shall is used to:
– offer help   *Shall I take that for you?* (Unit 8)
– ask for suggestions   *What shall we do this evening?* (Unit 13)
    What shall I buy? (Unit 13)

SHOULD and OUGHT TO (Unit 17)

Positive	Negative	Question
I should go.	I shouldn't go.	Should I go?
You ought to go.	You oughtn't to go.	Ought I to go?

In this book *should* and *ought to* are used to:
– ask for advice   *What should I do?*
    Should I take a sleeping pill?
– give advice   *He shouldn't work so late.*

MUST (Throughout, Unit 24)

In this book *must* is used to:
– express obligation   (throughout)
– draw conclusions   *They must be English.*

MAY and *MIGHT* (Units 8, 21, 24)

Positive
I may come late.
She might come late.

Negative
I may not arrive on time.
She might not arrive on time.

Question
May I use the phone?
(*May* here = polite request)

In this book *may* is used to:
– make polite requests   *May I use the phone?*   (Unit 8)
May and *might* are used to:
– talk about possible future events   *I may/might give her a ring.*   (Unit 21)
Might is used to:
– draw conclusions   *She might be American.*   (Unit 24)

WILL/WON'T (Units 11, 19, 33)

Positive
There'll be a lot of traffic.

Negative
There won't be much traffic.

Question
Will there be much traffic?

In this book *will/won't* are used:
– to talk about future predictions   *There'll be a lot of traffic on the M25.*   (Unit 11)
– to make promises   *We'll send you a postcard.*   (Unit 11)
– in predictions and promises combined   *I'll phone as soon as we get to France.*   (Unit 11)
  with time clauses beginning with *when* and
  as soon as
– to accept warnings and advice   *O.K. I will.*   (Unit 19)
  Don't worry. I won't.   (Unit 19)
– in first conditional *if* clauses   *If you come up too fast, your lungs will hurt.*   (Unit 33)

VERB *HAVE TO*   (Unit 7)

Present

Positive
You have to meet them at
  the station.

Negative
You don't have to meet them
  at the airport.

Question
Do you have to meet them?

Short answer
Positive
Yes, I do.

Short answer
Negative
No, I don't.

Past

Positive
I had to meet them at the
  station.

Negative
I didn't have to meet them
  at the airport.

Question
Did you have to meet them?

Short answer
Positive
Yes, I did.

Short answer
Negative
No, I didn't.

1 In this book *have to* is used to talk about duties and obligations.
2 Note that we use *do/does/did* to make the negative and question forms of *have to*, e.g. *he doesn't have to go/ do they have to go*. You cannot say: ~~he hasn't to go~~, or ~~have they to go~~.
3 *Don't have to/Doesn't have to* mean the same as *needn't*, i.e. there is **no** obligation to do something.
4 *Had to* is the past tense form of *have to, have got to* and *must*.
5 The use of *have to* often suggests that someone else is telling you what to do.

VERB *ALLOWED TO* (Unit 18)

Positive
You're allowed to smoke.

Negative
You're not allowed to smoke./You aren't
    allowed to smoke.

Question

Are you allowed to smoke?

Short answer
Positive
Yes, you are.

Short answer
Negative
No, you aren't

> 1 In this book *allowed to* is used to talk about permission, rules and laws.
> 2 *To be allowed to* is the passive form of the verb *to allow*.
> 3 *Allowed to* cannot usually be used with the impersonal pronoun *it*, i.e. you cannot say: It is allowed to smoke
>   but it can be used with the impersonal pronoun *you*, e.g. *You are allowed to smoke.*

VERB *USED TO* (Unit 31)

Positive
I used to live in that house.

Negative
I didn't use to live here.

Question

Did you use to live there?

Short answer
Positive
Yes, I did.

Short answer
Negative
No, I didn't.

> In this book *used to* is used to:
> – talk about past habits
> – talk about past situations
>
> *I used to speak Punjabi at home but I don't now.*
> *We didn't use to have a washing machine.*

REPORTED STATEMENTS (Unit 36)

Direct speech	**Reported speech**
'**I'm** thirty-five.' (Present simple)	He said that **he was** thirty-five. (Past simple)
'**I'm working** this evening.' (Present continuous)	She said that **she was working** this evening. (Past continuous)
'**I've been** here before.' (Present perfect)	She said that **she had been** there before. (Past perfect)
'**I met** him last year.' (Past simple)	She said that **she had met** him a year ago. (Past perfect)

but

I want to go home.' (Present simple)	He says **he wants** to go home. (Present simple)

> 1 When the tense of the main reporting verb is in the past, the tense of the reported speech is changed.
> 2 When the tense of the main reporting verb is in the present, there is no change of tense in the reported
>   speech.
> 3 *That* can be used after the main reporting verb, e.g. *He said (that) he wanted to go home.*

REPORTED QUESTIONS (Unit 38)

Direct speech	**Reported speech**
'How old are you?'	She asked (him) how old he was.
'Are you coming?'	She asked (him) if he was coming.
'Do you work in London?'	She asked me if I worked in London.

> 1 Tense changes in reported questions are the same as in reported statements.
> 2 The word order of the question in reported questions always changes, e.g.
>   *'Where are you going?' – He asked me where I was going.*
> 3 The auxiliary verbs *do/does/did* are not used in reported questions.

INDIRECT REQUESTS AND INSTRUCTIONS (Unit 22)

Positive
(Can/Could you) ask/tell her to phone back later (?)

Negative
(Can/Could you) ask/tell her not to phone me at work (?)

In this type of sentence, *ask* and *tell* are followed by an object plus an infinitive.

REPORTED REQUESTS AND COMMANDS (Unit 25)

Direct request

'Can
'Could | you come and see me?'

Reported request

She | wants | me | to go and see her.
would like	you
asked	him
	her
	us
	them

'Please don't phone me.'

She asked me not to phone her.

Direct command

'Talk to Bob.'
'Don't phone me.'

Reported command

She told me to talk to Bob.
She told me not to phone her.

1 Reported requests and commands are made by using verbs like: *want, would like, ask* and *tell* with an object and an infinitive.
2 You cannot say: ~~She wants that you come.~~
3 Note that *tell* must be followed by a personal direct object, e.g. *I told her to go home.*
 You cannot say: ~~I told to go home.~~

TIME CLAUSES IN THE PAST WITH *WHEN, WHILE, AFTER* AND *BEFORE* (Units 15, 20, 34)

When
When he arrived, he made a phone call.

In time clauses with *while, after* and *before*, the gerund with *-ing* can be used if the subject of both clauses is the same.

While
While we were camping in France, we saw a forest fire. *or*
While camping in France, we saw a forest fire. *but*
While **we** were camping in France, **he** arrived.

After
After driving/After he drove all night, he spent the day in bed. *but*
After **they** left, **he** went to bed.

Before
Before going to bed/Before she went to bed, she had a shower. *but*
Before **they** arrived, **she** made some coffee.

TIME CLAUSES IN THE FUTURE WITH *WHEN* AND *AS SOON AS* (Unit 11)

When he arrives, I'll ask him.
As soon as she phones, I'll let you know.

Although the main verb is expressed by a *will* future, the verb in the time clause stays in the present simple tense.

CONDITIONAL CLAUSES WITH *IF* (First conditional) (Unit 33)

If it rains, I'll take my umbrella.
If it rains, I won't come.
If it doesn't rain, we'll go to the beach.

In this book, the first conditional is used to:
- describe possible consequences   *If you come up too fast, your lungs will hurt.*
- threaten or warn people   *If you don't go away, I'll call the police.*

1 The first conditional is similar to time clauses in the future with *when* and *as soon as*. The main verb is expressed by a *will* future but the verb in the *if* clause stays in the present simple.
2 *If . . . not* is sometimes replaced by *unless*, e.g. *I won't come unless you really need me.*

CLAUSES OF CONTRAST WITH *ALTHOUGH* AND LINKING WORD *HOWEVER* (Unit 30)

Two contrasting sentences and ideas can be linked with *although*, e.g.
Although *some still live in the outback, many now live in cities and towns.*

The same idea can be expressed by using the linking word *however* at the beginning of the second sentence, e.g. *Some still live in the outback.* However, *many now live in cities and towns.*

CLAUSES OF RESULT WITH *SO/SUCH . . . THAT* (Unit 32)
I was so tired (that) I fell asleep.
It was such an amazing sight (that) I took a whole roll of film.

1 *So* and *such* are often followed by a clause of result beginning with *that*.
2 Sometimes the word *that* is omitted.
3 For differences between *so* and *such* see the *Degree* section of this Language review.

RELATIVE CLAUSES (Units 5, 10, 28)

Non-defining relative clauses (Unit 5)

Louisa, who's a nurse, lives in Oxford.
Merton College, which was founded in 1264, is one of the oldest Oxford colleges.
Isabel is at a language school, where she is studying for her FCE.

1 A non-defining relative clause adds more information to that in the main clause.
2 If the relative clause is in the middle of a sentence, there are usually commas around it. If it is at the end, there is usually a comma before it.

Defining relative clauses with *who, which* and *where* (Unit 10)

Robert Burns was a Scottish poet who wrote Auld Lang Syne.
Tartan is a cloth which has a special criss-cross pattern.
Harris is an island where they make tweed.

1 A defining relative clause defines the person, thing or place we are talking about.
2 There is no comma before a defining relative clause.

Relative clauses without *who, that* and *which* (Unit 28)

A German girl (whom/that) I know went to India for a holiday last year.

1 *Who, that* and *which* can be omitted if they are objects of the verb in the defining relative clause.
2 *Whom* is the object form of *who*. It is used in written English but rarely in spoken English.

COMPARISON OF ADJECTIVES (Unit 29)

1 Comparative adjectives are formed:
  – by adding -er to the end of shorter adjectives, e.g. *high – higher*.
  – by putting *more* or *less* in front of longer adjectives, e.g. *polluted – more polluted, expensive – less expensive*.
2 Comparative adjectives can be modified by adding intensifiers such as *much* and *a bit*, e.g. *much higher, a bit cheaper*.

COMPARISON OF ADVERBS (Unit 17)

Most comparative adverbs are formed by adding *more* to the adverb, e.g. *more often, more frequently, more slowly*. However, with short adverbs like *hard, early, late, fast*, the comparative is formed by adding -er, e.g. *harder, earlier, later*.

FREQUENCY (Unit 4)

Adverbial phrases

once	a week
twice	a fortnight
three times	a month
four times	a year

Adverbs

always	occasionally
usually	hardly ever
often	never
sometimes	

1 Adverbial phrases of frequency are usually positioned at the end of the relevant clause or sentence.
2 Adverbs of frequency are usually positioned before the main verb but after the verb *to be*.

STATIVE VERBS (Unit 23)

Certain verbs (stative verbs) can be used before adjectives and combined with *like* before a noun.

It sounds nice.
It looks delicious.
It feels good.
It tastes disgusting.
It smells strange.
It seems long.

It sounds like sizzling sausages.
It looks like juicy fruit.
It feels like home.
It tastes like sour milk.
It smells like fish.
It seems like a year.

QUANTITY (Units 12, 16)

Adjectives

All / Most / Many / Some / A few / Both / No   young people like big cities.

Pronouns

All / Most / Many / Some / A few / Both   (of them) like big cities.
None (of them) likes big cities.

Quantity words with countable nouns

too many / not many / a lot (of) / plenty (of) / (not) enough   people

Quantity words with uncountable nouns

too much / not much / a lot (of) / plenty (of) / (not) enough   food

DEGREE (Units 32, 37)

Adverbs of degree (Unit 37)

I'm very/rather/quite/fairly/a bit/
not at all shy.

> 1 Most adverbs of degree go before the words they modify.
> 2 -ly intensifiers can be used in place of *very*, e.g. *She's terribly kind.*

So/Such a . . . (Unit 32)

It's such a beautiful beach.
They're such beautiful animals.
It's so beautiful.

> 1 *Such* is used before an adjective plus a noun.
> 2 *So* is used before an adjective or an adverb.
> 3 Both *so* and *such* can be linked to a clause of result or consequence, e.g. *It was such an amazing sight (that) I took a whole roll of film.*

PREPOSITIONS

During (Unit 20)

He died during the war.
During a fit of madness, he cut off
his ear.

> *During* is used with a noun which says *when* something happened, not *how long*.
> It cannot be used in the same way as *for*.

ADJECTIVES WITH PREPOSITIONS (Unit 39)

Of   I'm frightened/afraid of the dark.
        I'm proud/ashamed of what I did.
About I'm angry/annoyed/upset about breaking the glass.
        I'm worried about Jenny.
With   I'm pleased/disappointed with my exam results.
        I'm bored/fed up with this book.
        I'm angry/annoyed with her.
At   I'm surprised/shocked at the news.
        I'm good/bad/hopeless at cooking.

REFLEXIVE PRONOUNS

myself   ourselves
yourself   yourselves
herself   themselves
himself
itself

> Reflexive pronouns are used when the subject and the object are the same person, e.g.
> *I had to live in conflict with myself.* (Unit 9)
> *He shot himself.* (Unit 20)

Irregular verbs

Verbs with no change

cost	cost	cost
cut	cut	cut
hit	hit	hit
hurt	hurt	hurt
let	let	let
put	put	put
shut	shut	shut

Verbs with one change

bring	brought	brought
build	built	built
buy	bought	bought
catch	caught	caught
feel	felt	felt
fight	fought	fought
find	found	found
get	got	got
have, has	had	had
hear	heard	heard
hold	held	held
keep	kept	kept
lead	led	led
learn	learnt	learnt
leave	left	left
lend	lent	lent
lose	lost	lost
make	made	made
mean	meant	meant
meet	met	met

pay	paid	paid
read /riːd/	read /red/	read /red/
say	said	said
sell	sold	sold
send	sent	sent
shine	shone	shone
shoot	shot	shot
sit	sat	sat
sleep	slept	slept
spend	spent	spent
stand	stood	stood
teach	taught	taught
tell	told	told
think	thought	thought
understand	understood	understood
win	won	won

Verbs with two changes

be (is, are)	was/were	been
begin	began	begun
bite	bit	bitten
blow	blew	blown
break	broke	broken
can	could	been able
choose	chose	chosen
come	came	come
do, does	did	done
draw	drew	drawn
drink	drank	drunk
drive	drove	driven

eat	ate	eaten
fall	fell	fallen
fly	flew	flown
forget	forgot	forgotten
freeze	froze	frozen
give	gave	given
go	went	gone
hide	hid	hidden
know	knew	known
lie	lay	lain
ring	rang	rung
run	ran	run
see	saw	seen
shake	shook	shaken
show	showed	shown
sing	sang	sung
sink	sank	sunk
speak	spoke	spoken
steal	stole	stolen
swim	swam	swum
take	took	taken
tear	tore	torn
throw	threw	thrown
wake	woke	woken
wear	wore	worn
write	wrote	written